Lost Newport

Lost Newport

VANISHED COTTAGES
OF THE RESORT ERA

THIRD EDITION, REVISED

Paul F. Miller

APPLEWOOD BOOKS
Carlisle, Massachusetts

Published in cooperation with
The Preservation Society of Newport County

An abbreviated version of this survey appeared in
Newport History: Journal of the Newport Historical Society
in the Fall 2005 and Spring 2006 issues.

ISBN 978-1-4290-9442-9

Thank you for purchasing an Applewood book.
Applewood reprints America's lively classics —
books from the past that are still of interest to
modern readers. For a free copy of our current
catalog, please write to Applewood Books,
P. O. Box 27, Carlisle, MA 01741.

www.awb.com

Book design by Barbara DaSilva and Diana Sibbald

Manufactured in the U.S.A.

TABLE OF CONTENTS

Introduction

*V*eteran world travelers visiting Newport, Rhode Island, in the first years of the twentieth century were as impressed as neophytes by the sheer concentration of opulent summer villas ringing this old colonial seaport. Grand Duke Boris of Russia's paean to the resort struck a characteristic chord: "I have never dreamed of such luxury as I have seen at Newport." Yet in the ranks of *habitués* of the cottage colony stood a few more-candid and prescient critics. Henry James in commenting on the disappearance of the pure spirit of the Newport of his youth lamented that "the white elephants, as one may best call them, all cry and no wool, all house and no garden, make now, for three or four miles, a barely interrupted chain…while their inverted owners, roused from a witless dream, wonder what in the world is to be done with them."

Within a few decades, James' observation would prove prophetic. Two world wars, a long depression, the introduction of a permanent income tax, high inheritance and real estate taxes, and the shortage of available domestic staff made Newport summer cottages, gradually and almost imperceptibly, anachronisms. With the evaporation of the market for large seasonal homes, the primary hope for the survival of these former cottages seemed in conversion to schools, as hauntingly evoked by Grace Kelly's Newport socialite character Tracy Lord in the 1956 Warner Bros. film *High Society*. And so, by the 1950s, much of the central Bellevue Avenue estate corridor was thus converted; nursing homes and apartment houses joined the ranks but educational institutions dominated, the chief landowners becoming Vernon Court Junior College, Salve Regina University, De La Salle Academy, St. Catherine's Academy, and Hatch Preparatory School. As not all summer houses could be saved, difficult choices had to be made, and were it not for these institutions much of Bellevue Avenue would have been cleared for new development and subdivision. This drastic response was the only rational move at the time to counter the loss of city tax revenues formerly generated by summer estates. Simultaneously, however, the city's economy moved away from dependency on the summer colony to hosting a major U.S. naval station with related defense industries. This, together with the

Great Villas Vanishing From Newport Scene

Newport Daily News,
March 19, 1973

commercial and residential development opportunities fostered by the completion of the Newport Bridge in 1969, ushered in an era of prosperous suburbanization.

Post–World War II prosperity also brought with it a desire for swift change, which, when faced with "redundant" architecture, proved merciless. The waterfront colonial street plan and wharves of Newport disappeared primarily in the late 1960s due to urban renewal and the creation of a new central arterial road designed to render downtown Newport more accessible to automobile traffic. In the process, however, local historic preservation movements reacted strongly and gained unprecedented impetus. Reaction had begun when Mrs. Katherine U. Warren and friends founded The Preservation Society of Newport County in 1945, initially to save the 1749 *Hunter House* from demolition for the extension of naval facilities. In 1968 Miss Doris Duke joined her with the creation of the Newport Restoration Foundation, which purchased and restored close to ninety primarily Colonial-era homes.

Market Square, looking north, ca. 1890

The success of such private preservation efforts is today so apparent that it is often taken for granted. To the first-time or casual visitor to Newport, a drive down the former main artery of the summer colony that is Bellevue Avenue still impresses with its seemingly uninterrupted alignment of exceptional nineteenth- and

Ocean House Hotel [1846], Russell Warren, architect

early-twentieth-century domestic architecture. On closer glimpse, or on foot, however, holes in the urban fabric can be detected. Virtually every block, and more so on the subsidiary cross streets, has lost a cottage of some local or frequently national merit. Although many were destroyed by fire, the majority of these homes were demolished for residential or commercial subdivision rather than lost to natural causes. Luckily, the very density of the cottage colony, with such an architectural *embarras de richesses*, masks such incursions.

This contextual density of cottage architecture is one of the unique facets of Newport. Unlike the rural country house model, the social and physical amenities of a landed seat did not apply here. The summer residents of Newport began by building freestanding, timber-framed cottages in the early nineteenth century, on what were essentially suburban-size lots ringing the existing colonial town. Minimally landscaped, these lots provided views across open meadows to the harbor or sea. The colony's social life was, at first, simple and literary: social life focused on the reception rooms of a handful of boardinghouses or hotels and a series of private clubs. As social and architectural ambitions grew, particularly after the Civil War, with an explosion of new fortunes in finance, industry, mining, and transit, the lot size rarely expanded. This led to the curious sight of progressively larger Beaux-Arts–style villas being erected on the site of earlier Gothic, Greek Revival, or Italianate cottages, with scant breathing room.

The scope of this survey is related to cottages built in the golden age of Newport's reign as the queen of resorts, roughly from 1830 to 1930. We will not consider, at this time, the many early cottages demolished during the Gilded Age to make way for larger, generally more architecturally significant houses on their sites. A large enough number of these earlier houses survives today to give us an impression of their charm, but they are noted more often for their formulaic construction. This is not to appear arbitrary nor to dismiss them altogether, for each, no doubt, was significant in its day and had important historical associations; witness the 1851 summer home of George Bancroft, historian and statesman, which hosted Bancroft's horticultural experiments to perfect the 'American Beauty' rose and meetings of the nation's literati, but which was leveled to make way for McKim, Mead & White's extraordinary *Rosecliff* of 1902.

Emphasis is given instead to those vanished cottages whose sites were either developed for structures not

Top: *Bancroft Cottage, demolished for Rosecliff*
Bottom: *Merritt Cottage, demolished for The Elms*

Oakland Farm, ca. 1906, Portsmouth, RI [demolished], country estate of Cornelius II and Alfred G. Vanderbilt

in sympathy with the earlier use of the lot or which were not replaced at all. Nor do we wish this survey to be viewed as comprehensive, for at present photographic evidence is lacking for a number of interesting vanished homes. It is hoped that with time such views will surface and also that any errors or omissions will be corrected through future research. We enthusiastically welcome such revision. It should also be pointed out that country estates, with farms, gardens, manor house and dependencies, stable and riding rings, and similar such amenities, did exist on the periphery of Newport, scattered across Aquidneck Island, with many dating back to the eighteenth century. Although acquired by such leading summer colonist families as the Taylors and Vanderbilts as a casual corollary to and closely interrelated with Newport social life, any listing of the farms would detract from the scope of a study of the cottage colony. Today these gentlemen's farms are a legacy largely lost to suburbanization.

Oakland Farm riding ring, ca. 1906 [demolished]

Although the following cottage inventory may seem to range stylistically from the ordinary to the sublime, it is the cumulative absence of these selected cottages from the grandeur of the ensemble that we aim to evoke. The ensemble seemed to teeter in the balance until the 1962 purchase by a group of friends, on behalf of the Preservation Society, of *The Elms*. This estate block, comprising the 1901 Beaux-Arts–style E. J. Berwind villa by architect Horace Trumbauer and a sizable formal garden, had been sold at public auction and was awaiting demolition. It constituted a major leap of faith for Mrs. Warren to intervene in saving a large early-twentieth-century cottage, knowing that its future would be dependent on funds generated by public visitation. Although the Society had been seasonally opening, under its auspices, Cornelius Vanderbilt II's *The Breakers* since 1947, the purchase of the Berwind property seemed to many to be tempting fate. The favorable public response amazed all who had heretofore felt that the Society should remain a guardian of Colonial Newport. In the following decade, eight more properties were acquired, through purchase and gift, all of them nineteenth-century summer homes in a range of styles; together they provide a comprehensive, contextual guide to the evolution of American domestic architecture, from the Colonial to the Beaux Arts. Strengthened further through adaptive reuse fostered by the condominium market, active in Newport since 1973, and historic district ordinances introduced in 1965, the future of the former cottage colony seems optimistic. Although it is logical to assume that additional great Newport cottages will fall victim to natural disaster or to economic downturns, it is hoped that knowing what previously stood on key sites and what contributed to making Newport a unique American architectural microcosm might remind inhabitants and visitors of the fragility of the surviving balance and perhaps inspire them to be sensitive to past architectural traditions in future construction.

Paul F. Miller, Curator
The Preservation Society of Newport County

COTTAGES OF
THE NORTH END

F. W. Andrews House by H. H. Richardson, ca. 1895

FRANK W. ANDREWS HOUSE *(1874)*
SUNSET LAWN
Andrews Estate
Henry Hobson Richardson, architect
Maple Avenue
Demolished

Engulfed by the 1940s expansion of the U.S. naval station, the Maple Avenue estate district was known in the nineteenth century for its sweeping views across open, sloping meadows to Narragansett Bay and surrounding countryside dotted with Colonial country seats and Revolutionary War earthworks. To embrace these views, Richardson (1838–86), assisted by Charles Follen McKim as draftsman, planned a cavernous Queen Anne–style summer home for retired importer of iron and crockery and real estate investor Frank William Andrews (1827–1903) and his wife, Maria Frances Adams Andrews, of 187 Beacon Street, Boston; Andrews was familiar with the architect's then simultaneous work at Trinity Church on Copley Square. For the house's exterior, the architect experimented with combinations of patterned shingles and clapboards. The Andrews villa's ground floor interior space centered around a living hall and comprised 6,000 square feet, then the largest floor plan of any Newport cottage. This structure became an important design source for the development of H. H. Richardson's Queen Anne style in such succeeding projects as the 1874–76 William Watts Sherman House in Newport. Following the death of Mrs. Andrews, the estate was inherited by her sons, Paul H. and Walter S. Andrews. Badly damaged by fire, the Andrews house was torn down in the mid-1920s and is now the site of a residential subdivision.

Castlewood, garden facade, ca. 1920

Castlewood, "Louis XVI" drawing room, ca. 1910

Castlewood, entrance facade, ca. 1906

HOUSE № 2

CASTLEWOOD *(1905)*
Bruguière-Hanan Estate
Edward Payson Whitman, architect
Maple Avenue and Girard Avenue
Demolished

Built on a 15-acre site including the highest land elevation at Codding-ton Point, this white glazed terra-cotta-trimmed brick Georgian villa, designed in neoclassical taste by Boston architect Edward P. Whitman, was visible from all of southern Narragansett Bay. Josephine S. Bruguière (1843–1915) of California, daughter of San Francisco banker Pedar Sather, founder of the Sather Banking Co., incorporated the remnants of an eighteenth-century earthenwork battery thought to have been erect-ed by the Comte de Rochambeau into the formal gardens. The interior featured high-style French and English reception rooms in Renaissance, Georgian, and Louis XV taste. Josephine Bruguière, remembered for her lavish entertaining, filed bankruptcy in August of 1914. Returning from Europe with her son Louis (1882–1954), she was drowned in the sinking of the White Star liner *Arabic*, torpedoed on August 19, 1915. Louis sur-vived and in 1948 married the widowed Margaret Louise Post Van Alen (1876–1969) of *Wakehurst* in Newport. *Castlewood* was sold to Arnold Watson Essex and then by his estate in 1916 to Mr. John Henry Hanan (1849–1920) of Brooklyn, New York, a millionaire shoe manufacturer.

Following Hanan's death in 1920, *Castlewood* was converted into an orphanage, the Mercy Home and School, and subsequently demolished by the U.S. government for World War II public housing for workers of the Newport torpedo and naval ordnance factories. A Louis XV–style paneled room was removed by Mr. Bruguière and stored; it has been since incorporated into a contemporary French house on Ocean Avenue.

Castlewood, entrance hall (top), dining room (middle), and salon (bottom), 1906

Philbrick Cottage, 1876

HOUSE N⁰·3

EDWARD S. PHILBRICK COTTAGE *(1874)*
Philbrick Estate
Coddington Point
S. J. Brown, architect
Demolished

During the 1870s, the shore at Coddington Point, a somewhat secluded but desirable waterfront locale, witnessed the construction of a series of picturesque villas along a new shore road called Coddington Avenue, serviced by a depot of the Old Colony Railroad. Chief among them was the 1874 Philbrick House, a gable-roofed Stick Style timber-framed cottage built by the Boston architect S. J. Brown for Edward Southwick Philbrick (1827–89) of Boston, an educator with the New England Freedmen's Aid Society during the Civil War and later a noted sanitary engineer. Sold in December 1899 to Theresa D. Weld (1873–1968, Mrs. Alfred Winsor

Weld) of Newton, Massachusetts, the property was, together with the nearby villas of Hugh L. Willoughby and C. Francis Bates, requisitioned by the city of Newport for expansion of the Newport naval station. Sold in August 1918 to the city of Newport for one dollar, the cottage was demolished and the site transferred to the United States government for naval purposes.

Bannister House, east facade, ca. 1955

Bannister House, 1947

HOUSE N⁰·4

JOHN BANNISTER HOUSE (CA. 1756)
Bannister-MacKaye Estate
West Main Road
(located just past the Newport-Middletown city line)
Demolished

This distinguished mid-eighteenth-century rusticated Georgian country house on West Main Road was built for Colonial architect Peter Harrison's brother-in-law, the merchant John Bannister (1707–67) and was likely renovated by Harrison. The property was acquired from Bannister by George Irish (1729–1801), who occupied the main house and farmed the land; his descendants in the Irish-MacKaye-Atwood family retained ownership until 1953, when the then unoccupied house was demolished for an elementary school. Salvaged interiors including the center hall archway and the main stair were acquired by Henry Francis du Pont for his Winterthur Museum in Delaware from Mary Goodwin MacKaye Atwood (1892–1986) in 1957.

Dudley Place, ca. 1920

HOUSE N°· 5

CHARLES DUDLEY HOUSE (CA. 1750)
Dudley-Bull-Church Estate
Attributed to Peter Harrison, architect
West Main Road at Miantonomi Avenue
(city line at One Mile Corner)
Demolished

Built as a country retreat for Royal Customs Collector Charles Dudley (d.1790), this square three-story house of wood painted and sanded to resemble stone was one of Colonial Newport's most architecturally distinguished domestic structures. The upper two stories were treated in the manner of a neoclassical rusticated pavilion decorated with Ionic pilasters rising to a low-hipped roof. Long associated, in the nineteenth century, with the Bull family of Newport, descendants of Henry Bull, one of the city's 1639 founders, the house was baptized *Dudley Place* under their ownership and converted to a summer residence. In 1882–83 McKim, Mead & White, architects, renovated the historic house for Charles M. Bull and Henry B. Bull VII. In 1894, Henry's son, noted New York surgeon Dr. William Tillinghast Bull (1849–1909), and wife, Marie Nevins Blaine, renewed the tradition of seasonally occupying the homestead. The property saw a further renaissance when purchased in 1927 by William K. Vanderbilt Jr. for his daughter Muriel Fair Vanderbilt (1900–72), then Mrs. Frederic Cameron Church Jr. and subsequently Mrs. Henry D. Phelps. A riding ring and stable were added to the rear of the estate for Mrs. Phelps, a lifelong equestrienne. *Dudley Place* was closed in 1936 when Muriel Vanderbilt moved to California following a divorce from Mr. Phelps. Upon her return following World War II, the

vicinity had become commercialized by the expansion of the nearby
U.S. naval base, and the property was left abandoned until sold for demolition in 1953. A gas station, a motel, and several residential subdivi-
sions now occupy the site, although the stable block was spared and has
been rehabilitated as condominium residences.

Dudley Place, Broadway at Miantonomi Avenue, ca. 1910

Hunter-Dunn House, ca. 1914

HOUSE N⁰· 6

HUNTER-DUNN HOUSE (1878)
George Champlin Mason & Son, architects
Training Station Road
Demolished

On retirement from the navy, Newport native Captain Charles Hunter (1813–73), son of Senator William Hunter and Mary Robinson Hunter of the colonial Hunter House on Washington Street, invested in waterfront farmland just north of the city's Point district. Hunter, then residing with his family in town at 12 Kay Street, did not get to develop the land as he returned to naval service with the outbreak of the Civil War. The Captain's overzealous initiative in pursuing a British ship with Confederate cargo into Cuban waters led to a second retirement in 1863. In November 1873, Hunter, his wife, Mary Rotch Hunter (1823–73), and three of his four daughters embarked on the transatlantic steamship *Ville du Havre* for France, intending to spend the winter on the Riviera. In the early morning hours of November 22, the steamer collided with the ironclad clipper ship Loch Earn. Mr. and Mrs. Charles Hunter and their daughter Caroline were lost in the sinking. Their daughters Mary and Anna Hunter survived by clinging to wreckage on their father's orders.

Eldest child Kate Hunter (1849–1930) had remained at home that season due to her recent marriage to Newport China Trader and future director of the regional Old Colony Railroad, Thomas Dunn (1834–1916). While her younger surviving sisters were raised by King family relatives, Kate Dunn resided at her father's Kay Street house until she hired George Champlin Mason & Son, Newport architects, to build a sizable new home on her share of the Hunter lands. Begun in 1877 and completed by the autumn of 1878, the waterside villa was a fieldstone and brick-accented Queen Anne style cottage with bracketed trim and interiors furnished by George E. Vernon of Newport. In 1896, Kate Hunter Dunn decided to sell the estate to Dr. Oliver Whipple Huntington, a Harvard professor of mineralogy and chemistry who would found the Cloyne School, a boarding school for boys, based in the house, rebaptized *Cloyne House*. Named after George Berkeley (1685–1753), the lord bishop of Cloyne, who had spent the years 1729 to 1732 at nearby *Whitehall* in Middletown, the institution was cofounded with educator

Hunter-Dunn Estate as St. Michael's School, 1940

and antiques collector Arthur Leslie Green (1864–1949), who acted as headmaster. Between 1914 and 1918, the naval station at Newport expanded outward from Coasters Harbor Island to Coddington Point and the northern section of the Point itself. Despite the increased traffic and construction around the Cloyne School, it persisted in operation until finally closed in 1920. At the auction of the school's assets, Arthur Leslie Green bought most of the property and in 1938 donated the land and Hunter-Dunn house to the Episcopal Diocese of Providence so that the Cloyne School might be reborn as the rechartered St. Michael's School. Alas, by the summer of 1942, it became apparent that the naval station's expansion and security would require seizure of the school property. With $75,000 in compensation, the land was condemned and repurposed and the Hunter-Dunn house demolished that year for naval housing and offices. St. Michael's School moved later, in 1943, to the former Rhode Island Avenue estate of the Misses Mason.

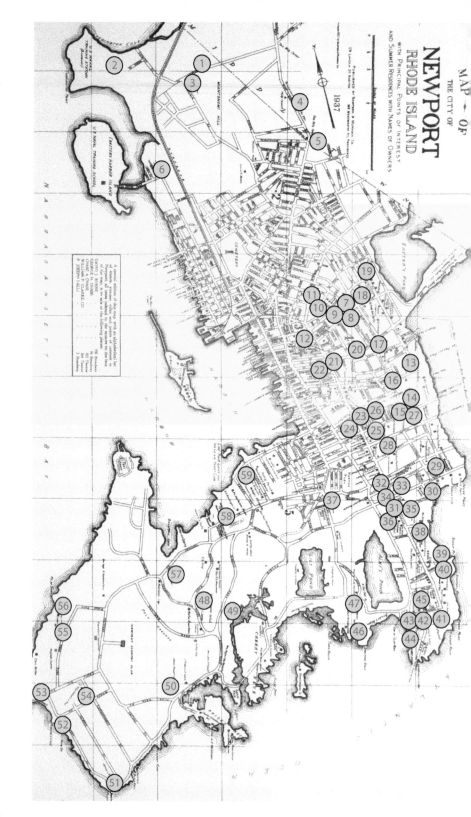

COTTAGES OF CENTRAL NEWPORT

Whitehall, ca. 1900

Whitehall, in a derelict state, ca. 1930

Whitehall, ca. 1897

HOUSE N^{O.} 7

WHITEHALL *(1894)*
King-Coogan Estate
McKim, Mead & White, architects
Catherine Street and Rhode Island Avenue
Demolished

Whitehall, built on the site of the former General Henry Van Rens-selaer cottage, was designed by McKim, Mead & White in their newly popular Colonial Revival style for a favorite client, New York building contractor and developer David H. King (1850–1916). King's New York construction projects included the pedestal base of the Statue of Liberty (1884); McKim, Mead & White's Madison Square Garden (1890); and the enlarged Cornelius Vanderbilt II residence at West Fifty-seventh Street (1894). In 1903, the estate was purchased by New York real estate baron, lawyer, and politician James Jay Coogan (1846–1915) of 599 Fifth Avenue. Coogan, Manhattan's first borough president, used the estate every season until the house was seriously damaged by fire on March 10, 1911. Due to the simultaneous remodeling of the family's Fifth Avenue residence, restoration work in Newport was postponed. With the 1915 death of Mr. Coogan, the house was to become unoccupied. Although the family remained sentimentally attached to the estate, major repairs never advanced, and this led to the pervasive legend that the Coogans had been snubbed socially, having issued invitations for a dinner party to which no one came. In point of fact, Mrs. Coogan, the former Harriet Gardiner Lynch (1862–1947) was socially prominent; as a great-granddaughter of John Lyon Gardiner, she inherited a very large section of the upper end of Manhattan. The Newport property was sold by Mrs. Coogan's son Jay on January 8, 1953, for $23,000 to Albert K. Sherman of Newport, who demolished the house that year for a residential subdivision.

The Corners, ca. 1935

HOUSE N⁰· 8

THE CORNERS *(1872)*
Cushman-Darlington Estate
Richard Morris Hunt, architect
49 Catherine Street
Demolished

Built by Hunt (1827–95) for a bohemian friend, the Boston-born actress and dramatic reader Charlotte Cushman (1816–76), *The Corners* was amongst the most ambitious of the architect's four picturesque "Swiss chalets" along the Catherine Street corridor. With its dramatically corbeled attic balcony, asymmetrical entrance tower, boldly articulated Stick Style trim, and outswept veranda, the Cushman villa dominated the intersection with Rhode Island Avenue in the then artistic-literary heart of the cottage colony. Sold by Miss Cushman's estate in 1890 to Bishop James H. (1856–1930) and Ella L. B. Darlington, the property passed to Rev. Henry V. B. Darlington and remained intact until subsequent sale to Bernice H. (Mrs. Mason D.) Rector (1909–86) in 1938. Severely damaged shortly thereafter by a fire, the house was demolished and contemporary homes built on the site in the 1950s.

HOUSE N⁰· 9

THOMAS G. APPLETON HOUSE *(1871)*
Appleton-Gibbes-Willard Estate
Richard Morris Hunt, architect
Catherine Street
Demolished

Thomas Gold Appleton (1812–84) of Boston, writer, artist, patron, ra-
conteur, and brother-in-law of Henry Wadsworth Longfellow, was a
long-standing friend of Hunt's and commissioned this highly original
and picturesque summer house in the immediate vicinity of Richard
and Catherine Hunt's own cottage. The most fully developed of Hunt's
"chalets," the Appleton House was known for its projecting balconies;
variously shaped dormers; painted shingle roof; and a profusion of posts,
brackets, and diagonal braces. The second story included wood shingles
and colored slate laid in patterns reminiscent of contemporary suburban
French villa architecture. The cottage was sold by Appleton's estate on
July 30, 1887, to Emma E. Barrett (1859–1905); then to Zela Gibbes
(1836–1907), under whose tenure the house was known as *Fair Haven*; and in 1907 to retired military engineer Colonel Joseph H. Willard
(1844–1933). Willard was active in civic affairs as a director of the Redwood Library and Newport Park Commission. Inherited by Willard's
daughters, the cottage was heavily damaged by fire and demolished in
the mid-1930s. The site was incorporated into the grounds of the adjoining *Ayrault House* and later subdivided.

Left: T. G. Appleton House, ca. 1875

Appleton House–Fair Haven, west facade, ca. 1912

Appleton House–Fair Haven, street facade, ca. 1912

Richardson Cottage, ca. 1875

HOUSE N^{O.} 10

GEORGE C. RICHARDSON HOUSE *(1871)*
Richardson Estate
Richard Morris Hunt, architect
Catherine Street
Demolished

Built on the lot between the Appleton and Cushman cottages, the George C. Richardson cottage was the summer residence of Boston financier, merchant and mayor of Cambridge George C. Richardson (1808-86) of G. C. Richardson & Co., a friend of Thomas G. Appleton and fellow bachelor. The villa was designed by Richard Morris Hunt as a foil to the neighboring Appleton and Cushman houses. A timber-framed chalet with Stick Style trim and mansard roof, the house boasted a wide bracketed veranda and a picturesque rear tower. Sadly the Richardson house, which rounded out the Hunt-designed block, was destroyed by fire within a decade of construction. The cottage was bought in 1873 by Newport real estate speculator, tailor and state legislator Daniel Tilley Swinburne (1819-74), and the vacant property was subsequently sold by his estate to Virginia Scott Hoyt (1867-1938), who in 1915 erected a stately, brick neo-Georgian house on the site by Cross & Cross, architects, known as *Ayrault House*.

Caldwell House, entrance hall as redecorated by J. D. Johnston, ca. 1890

HOUSE N°. 11

CALDWELL HOUSE *(CA. 1855)*

Misses Caldwell Estate
Kay and Ayrault Streets
Demolished

Built as the summer residence of Boston dry goods merchant Caleb Chace (d.1862), this Italianate summer cottage was acquired by William Shakespeare Caldwell (1821–71) of New York and Louisville, Kentucky, in 1866. Caldwell founded and controlled gas companies that lit a number of southern and midwestern cities, including Louisville, Mobile, New Orleans, Cincinnati, and St. Louis. In 1890, his orphaned daughters, Mary Gwendoline Byrd Caldwell (1863–1909), later the Marquise des Monstiers-Mérenville, and Mary Elizabeth Breckenridge Caldwell (1865–1910), later the Baroness Kurt von Zedtwitz, commissioned a private chapel and a music room, both decorated with stained and opalescent glass windows by John La Farge (1835–1910), as part of alterations undertaken by the Newport architect John Dixon Johnston (1849–1928). On April 20, 1931, Waldemar Conrad von Zedtwitz, the sisters' sole heir, sold the house which was promptly demolished for a residential subdivision. The chapel's stained glass was purchased by the Diocese of Fall River, Massachusetts, and incorporated into St. Patrick's Convent in that city. In 2004, Salve Regina University acquired the glass from the diocese and returned the windows to Newport for installation in a new campus chapel by Robert A. M. Stern (2010).

Hill Top, ca. 1890

HILL TOP *(CA. 1830/1869)*
Gilliat-Hunt Estate
Bellevue Avenue at Touro Street
Demolished

In 1856, American Barbizon painter William Morris Hunt (1824–79) and his wife, China Trade heiress Louisa D. Perkins (1831–97), purchased the Greek Revival home of John H. Gilliat (1807–73) at the intersection of Touro Street and Bellevue Avenue. Known as *Hill Top*, the house had been built as the two-story cottage of retired Baltimore merchant Valentine Henry "Harry" Schroeder (1787–1870), of the firm of Schley & Schroeder, and his wife, Henrietta Maria Ghequiere (1790–1877). In 1831, the Schroeders' daughter, Susan Harriett (1812–46), married Richmond importer and tobacco dealer John Gilliat, and as their family grew, they were given *Hill Top* in the 1840s. Following the 1856 sale, the Gilliat family moved to *Vaucluse* in nearby Portsmouth.

William M. Hunt had come to Newport to socialize with friends from the Boston artistic and literary set he favored—Louis G. Agassiz, Thomas G. Appleton, Henry Wadsworth Longfellow—and to open a teaching studio. The house was set back in a large yard on the periphery of the old town with plantings of specimen trees around it. In 1858 Hunt built a two-story stable with classroom and upstairs studio in the rear of the garden; the studio soon attracted such future luminaries as John La Farge and William and Henry James. During the summer of 1860, younger brother, budding architect Richard Morris Hunt (1827–95), came up from New York to recover from dysentery and stayed at the nearby Fillmore Hotel. Strolling one day near his brother's cottage, R. M. Hunt met Catharine Howland (1841–1909), daughter of successful shipping firm director Samuel Shaw Howland. A courtship ensued and the couple married in 1861. William Morris Hunt decided, in 1862, to move back to Boston in search of better artistic and teaching opportunities, and in 1863 he sold *Hill Top* to Richard and Catharine. The cottage and studio then became a center of Newport cultural and social life, and Richard used the studio for his own burgeoning architectural practice. Alterations occurred between 1869–70 and 1877–78 with the addition of an upper story and Doric-order loggia and portico. Following Catherine Hunt's death in 1909, the cottage and its sizeable lot were sold by the family and converted into the Hilltop Inn. The studio was, in 1912, appropriately remodeled and leased as the first headquarters of the Newport Art Association, until the association's purchase of the Hunt-designed 1863 J. N. A. Griswold House in 1916. *Hill Top* and its inn outbuildings were demolished in 1925 to make way for the Viking Hotel opened in 1926 on the placement of the Hunt cottage.

WILLIAM GAMMELL COTTAGE *(CA. 1872)*

Gammell Estate
The Cliffs
Demolished

Built for William Gammell II (1812–89), a distinguished professor of belles lettres, history, and rhetoric at Brown University in Providence, this large Italianate cottage with fanciful bracketed eaves was built by Gammell following his marriage to Elizabeth Amory Ives (1830–97) on Ives family land along the cliffs immediately to the north of the cottage of his father-in-law, Robert Hale Ives (1798-1875). Ives, active in the family trading firm of Brown & Ives in Providence, was a founder of both the Rhode Island and Butler Hospitals in Providence. Known in the resultant Ives-Gammell family compound as *North House*, the timber-framed house was torn down by the widowed Elizabeth Ives Gammell in 1889 to be replaced with a brick and masonry Queen Anne– and Tudor-style villa known as *Ocean Lawn* (extant) by architects Peabody & Stearns. Daughter Elizabeth Hope Gammell Slater (1854–1944) would similarly build a Peabody & Stearns brick Georgian villa called *Hopedene* on cliff-front family land in 1902. Son Robert Ives Gammell inherited his grandfather Ives' residence, *South Cottage*, or *Southside*, at the end of Narragansett Avenue; similar in scale and style to *North House*, it too was demolished, in 1955, and its site incorporated into the *Ocean Lawn* property by then owners Mr. and Mrs. Harvey S. Firestone.

Left: *Gammell Cottage, ca. 1910*

H. A. C. Taylor House, garden façade, ca. 1910

HOUSE Nº· 14

H. A. C. TAYLOR HOUSE *(1886)*
Taylor Estate
McKim, Mead & White, architects
Annandale Road
Demolished

An icon of Colonial Revival architecture in America, McKim, Mead & White's internationally celebrated cottage for Henry Augustus Coit Taylor (1841–1921) of New York initiated the Adamseque "Colonial" design that continued through the Second World War and, in an abridged fashion, survives in America to the present. Taylor was a highly successful financier and director of National City Bank and the family firm of Moses Taylor & Co. Following the death of his wife, Charlotte Talbot Fearing Taylor (1845–99), H. A. C. Taylor began to spend more time outside Newport at *The Glen*, his nearby 700-acre Portsmouth farm, where on the eve of his death he commissioned plans for an eighteenth-century French-style chateau from architect John Russell Pope (1874–1937). Taylor's son,

Left: *H.A.C. Taylor House, entrance façade, 1887*

Moses Taylor V (1871–1928), and his wife, Edith Bishop Taylor Nicholson (1874–1959), would prefer life at *The Glen* to the Newport cottage. Frequently sublet, the house remained in the family until its sale by Moses Taylor's surviving son, Francis Bishop Taylor (1900–67), on October 15, 1952, to Barbara L. Holmsen. That year the cottage was demolished for subdivision of its grounds. Some architectural salvage was incorporated into the adjacent outbuildings of *Ocean Lawn* and into a Colonial Revival subdivision, Johnson Terrace, then under construction on East Main Road in Middletown.

H. A. C. Taylor House, portico, ca. 1947

H. A. C. Taylor House, ca. 1947

Cliffs, ca. 1875

HOUSE N⁰. 15

THE FEARING COTTAGE [CLIFFS] *(1859)*
Daniel Fearing House
George Champlin Mason, architect (?)
Narragansett Avenue at Annandale Road
Demolished

This large timber-framed Italianate house was built for prosperous New York banker and merchant Daniel Butler Fearing (1804–70) and his wife, Harriet Richmond Fearing (1810–71), who owned, like their neighbors the Iveses, a large tract of land on the cliffs. The cottage passed to his son Henry Seymour Fearing (1832–86) and his wife, Serena Mason Jones (d. 1880), and then to H. S. Fearing's son, bibliophile and mayor of Newport Daniel B. Fearing (1859–1918). Henry Seymour Fearing's siblings built their own houses on family land in immediate proximity to their father's cottage. In 1871–72, George Richmond Fearing (1839–1920) and his wife, the former Harriet Travers, built *The Orchard*, one of Newport's earliest high-style French villas, on a parcel facing Narragansett Avenue and the home of his father-in-law, William R. Travers (see page 85); George Fearing likely selected the design for this villa from a volume in Hunt's French architectural library, probably César Daly's 1864 *L'Architecture privée au XIXe siècle*, Vol. 3, while the architect was working between 1869 and 1872 on the Travers house for his in-laws. Immediately to the west of *The Orchard* rose the cottage of sister Amey Richmond Fearing Sheldon (1834–1908), while to the north sister Charlotte Talbot Fearing Taylor (1845–99) would build the H. A. C. Taylor house with her husband. The ancestral Fearing cottage was inherited by nephew Moses Taylor V, to be consolidated within his neighboring property. Taylor's heirs demolished the house following World War II to reduce tax liabilities.

The Fearing Cottage, croquet party, ca. 1865

Sheldon Cottage, ca. 1875

HOUSE Nᴼ· 16

FREDERICK SHELDON HOUSE *(CA. 1860)*
Sheldon Estate
George Champlin Mason, architect
Annandale Road
Demolished

With its broad veranda, low-hipped mansard roof, and projecting rear
service ell, this Italianate cottage for New York bibliophile and yachts-
man Frederick Sheldon (1821–1907) was typical of local architect
George Champlin Mason's summer cottages. A virtual development by
him arose in the 1860s for the extended Fearing family in the vicinity of
Narragansett Avenue and the cliffs. Mrs. Sheldon was the former Amey
Richmond Fearing (1834–1908); having no children, she left a bequest
to the library at Harvard and the house to nephew George R. Fearing,
Jr. (1871–1956) who combined the property with his father's adjoining
estate *The Orchard* and in whose hands it remained until eventual demolition following World War II.

HOUSE Nᴼ· 17

BEACH CLIFFE *(1852)*
DeLancey Kane–Peterson-Mattison Estate
Detlef Lienau and Léon Marcotte, architects
Bath Road (now Memorial Boulevard)
between Annandale Road and Cliff Street
Demolished

With *Beaulieu, Château-sur-Mer, Fairlawn, Malbone,* and *Stone Villa,* the DeLancey Kane estate *Beach Cliffe* was the most opulent of pre–Civil War Newport villas and the first modern French château in the city. The German-born, Paris-trained Lienau (1818–87) formed a partnership with the French-born, New York–based cabinetmaker/decorator Marcotte (1824–87) between 1851 and 1854. *Beach Cliffe* resulted from this collaboration, and with its French Second Empire facades and cosmopolitan Louis XV–style academic interiors was decades ahead of its time. Set in almost twenty acres of a Romantic landscape park designed by R. B. Leuchars of New Haven, in close proximity to the public beach, the estate set a new standard for the fashionable house and garden. Home to New York sportsman Oliver DeLancey Kane (1816–74) and his wife, née Louisa Astor Langdon (1821–94), a granddaughter of John Jacob Astor, it reinforced their status as leaders of the Newport–New York social set. Kane brought the first four-in-hand road coach, *Tallyho,* from England to America, and with it came the sport of road coaching to Newport. The estate was sold in 1867 to the Philadelphia author and publisher Charles Jacobs Peterson (1818–87) and later to Richard Van-

Left: *Beach Cliffe, ca. 1875*

[51]

selous Mattison (1851–1936), the "asbestos king." In 1939, Eugene J. O'Reilly (1914–2008) bought the property, by then rebaptized *Bushy Park*, for $12,000 and subsequently demolished the main house to subdivide the property. Both the gatehouse (ca. 1859), by Newport architect Seth Bradford, facing Memorial Boulevard, and the carriage house (ca. 1895) on Annandale Road, however, survive as does Lienau's 1864 Lockwood-Matthews mansion in Norwalk, Connecticut; with its interiors by Marcotte and Herter Brothers, it provides a glimpse of the then fashionable Second Empire artistic interiors that were the glory of *Beach Cliffe*.

Linden Gate, ca. 1947

HOUSE N⁰· 18

LINDEN GATE *(1873)*
Henry G. Marquand House
Richard Morris Hunt, architect
Rhode Island Avenue and Old Beach Road
Demolished

Built as the summer residence of H. G. Marquand (1819–1902), an art patron and successful New York investor in banking, railroads, and real estate, *Linden Gate* was a large picturesque Swiss chalet gone baronial; built of random-coursed ashlar, diamond-patterned red and black brick, and upper stories of half-timbering with intricate bargeboards. The interior featured a paneled room by Hunt's collaborator, the Florentine sculptor Luigi Frullini, and interior decoration by John La Farge and Samuel Colman. Mr. Marquand, a leading philanthropist, was also the president of the board of trustees of the Metropolitan Museum of Art, a longtime friend of Hunt, and an inveterate collector. So crammed with ceramics, textiles, and antiques were the interiors of *Linden Gate* that contemporaries labeled the house "Bric-a-Brac Hall." It was to *Linden Gate* that artist John Singer Sargent came from London in 1887, at Henry Marquand's insistence, to paint his wife, the former Elizabeth Allen

Linden Gate, main facade (top), *ca. 1880,
and garden facade* (bottom), *ca. 1897*

(1826–95), on only his second visit to the United States; the resultant success of this and other Newport client portraits helped to launch the painter's American career as a portraitist. The property was maintained by Marquand's daughter and son-in-law, Rev. and Mrs. Roderick Terry (Linda Marquand, 1852–1931), until sold by their estate in 1951. Converted to apartments and offices, the house was severely damaged by fire on February 18, 1973. Some reception room paneling, including elements by Frullini, was salvaged and *Linden Gate* was demolished for a residential subdivision.

Linden Gate, reception room, ca. 1883

Linden Gate, stair and entrance hall, 1951

*Linden Gate, east facade or garden facade with Roderick Terry's
1913 music room addition, 1969*

Pumpelly Cottage, ca. 1885

HOUSE Nᵒ· 19

PUMPELLY COTTAGE *(1881)*
Pumpelly Estate
Calvert Vaux, architect
Gibbs Avenue between Catherine and Francis Streets
Demolished

This three-story Stick Style chalet with Orientalist trim appeared every bit as urbane as Raphael Pumpelly (1837–1923), the successful geologist, explorer, and world traveler who commissioned it from his friend Vaux. Associated with Newport's scientific and literary societies, Pumpelly was a much-loved member of both the intellectual and social sets of the town. With expansive views from its verandas to Easton's Pond and the sea beyond, the house appeared like an exotic gypsy wagon on the heights of Gibbs Avenue. Following Pumpelly's death in 1923 the eclectic house was sold by his heirs in April 1924 to a neighbor, Julia W. Emmons, to be incorporated into her estate. The house, damaged by fire in 1920, was demolished and contemporary homes later built on the site.

Pumpelly Cottage, street view, ca. 1890

Ladd Villa, street facade, ca. 1897

HOUSE N⁰· 20

LADD VILLA *(CA. 1865)*
Ladd Estate
John G. Ladd, builder
Bath Road (now Memorial Boulevard)
Demolished

Built by prosperous Newport architect and contractor John G. Ladd
(1806-1890) and his wife, Phebe A. Watson Ladd, as a private residence,
this rambling timber-framed, cupola-clad Italianate villa was continually
added to by Ladd as a professional calling card, witnessed by the projecting ells. Set far back from Bath Road, when this section of the city
was regarded as highly desirable, the Ladd family continued in residence
until 1910, when the surviving heir, Maude Ladd Scott, sold the house
to Messrs. Hirsch and Hyman, Providence developers. With the then
pending widening of Bath Road about to commence, plans were made
to build bungalows on the grounds. On May 16, 1911, fire ravaged the
house. Plans to repair the structure were abandoned, and in March of
1912 the property was sold to Rhode Island Senator George P. Wetmore
for demolition; he acquired the land primarily to hasten the widening of Bath Road as part of a civic beautification campaign. The site
was rezoned for twenty-four building lots, and the Memorial Boulevard
frontage is now commercial.

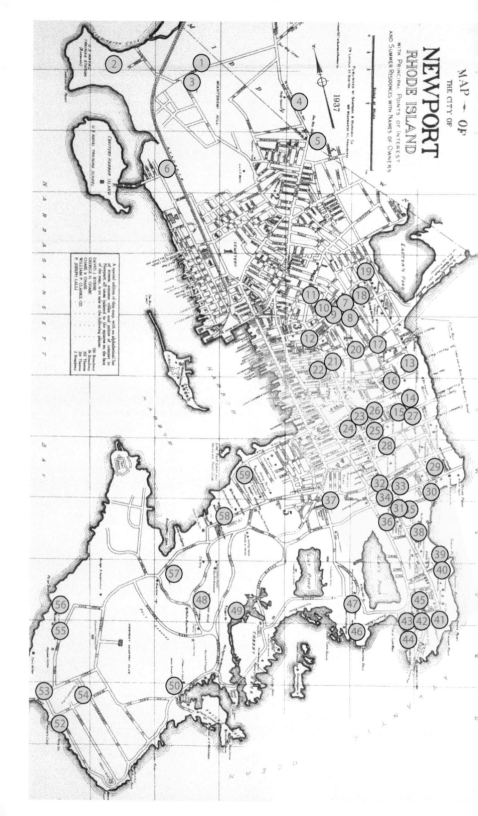

COTTAGES OF
BELLEVUE AVENUE

Top: *Stone Villa, street facade, ca. 1957*
Bottom: *Stone Villa, watercolor of garden facade
by Mstislav Dobujinsky, 1949*

Stone Villa, ca. 1920

HOUSE N⁰· 21

STONE VILLA *(CA. 1832–1835, ALTERATIONS CA. 1885)*
Middleton-Brooks-Bennett-Whitehouse Estate
Alexander McGregor, McIntosh & Alger, builder-architects
Bellevue Avenue between Jones Avenue and William Street
Demolished

In 1835, Henry Middleton (1770-1846), a rice planter of Charleston, South Carolina and husband of the former Mary Helen Hering (1772-1850), bought this impressively-scaled fieldstone and granite-trimmed Italianate villa from local builder Alexander McGregor. Middleton, the son of Arthur Middleton, signer of the Declaration of Independence, and Esther Mary Izard, was also the owner of the Middleton Place plantation on the Ashley River outside Charleston. The new house he acquired near the beginning of Bellevue Avenue was sited at the crest of a hill and offered then open, tree-less views across meadows to the bay to the west and the beach to the east. From one of South Carolina's most prominent families, Middleton served his native state as governor and two-term congressman and was later appointed ambassador to Russia.

The Middleton residence, then one of the town's largest homes, disingenuously named *Stone Villa*, quickly became a gathering place for the extended Izard and Middleton families then summering in Newport and environs. First cousin Arthur Middleton (1785–1837) and his wife, Alicia, daughter of Charleston merchant Nathaniel Russell, acquired their own nearby Newport cottage; their son Nathaniel Russell Middleton (1810–90) married Anna Elizabeth DeWolf (1815–1908) of *Hey Bonnie Hall* in Bristol, Rhode Island, and would reside there. Another first cousin, Henry Augustus Middleton (1793–1887), and his wife, the former Harriott Kinloch, also became Newport summer residents. The daughter of *Stone Villa*'s Henry Middleton, Maria Middleton Pringle, died with her husband and two children in the sinking of the steamship *Pulaski*, together with other southern summer residents including the Hamilton family and Hugh Swinton Ball, with his wife, Marianna Channing Ball, en route from Charleston to Newport on June 14, 1838. The tragedy deeply scarred the resort community.

With the advent of war, *Stone Villa* was placed in the guardianship of a northern son-in-law, John Hunter, and then sold to Sidney Brooks (1799–1878) of Boston and his wife, the former Frances Dehon (1805–71), a cousin of the Middletons and Russells. Brooks, a Boston and New York financier, expanded the house in the 1860s and adorned it with works by his friend the Florence-based American sculptor Hiram Powers, for whom he acted as agent. Following Sidney Brooks' death, *Stone Villa* was sold to publisher and sportsman James Gordon Bennett Jr. (1841–1918), who had been renting cottages in town since 1875.

Purchased for $32,500 from the Brooks estate, the *Newport Mercury* of August 30, 1879, reported the rumor that it was Mr. Bennett's intention to make the Middleton-Brooks villa into a new clubhouse. The publisher had bought property on Cliff Street in 1877 for the construction of summer rental cottages as part of long-standing plans for real estate development in the resort. Socially, his active role in the community's sporting life, as an organizer of the first polo matches, the local coaching club, gun club, and later the country club, was widely known. Although Bennett may have had the intention of converting the house or replacing it with something modern by his architect friends in the new firm of McKim, Mead & White, he opted out of such a scheme that summer when the decision was made to launch the construction of an innovative new social center directly across the street, the Newport Casino (1879–81)—a decision that had nothing to do with the perceived slight to Captain Henry Augustus Candy of the Ninth Queen's Royal Lancers (retired).

Candy had been recruited in England by Bennett to teach polo to a Newport team during the 1879 season. Captain Candy, to whom seasonal membership in the established Newport Reading Room had been extended, was riding past the reading room in early August when a member challenged him to ride his pony into the club; this Candy did with poise. The prank caused offense to the club's governors and the invitation extended to Captain Candy was revoked. It is an all-pervasive Newport legend that the matter was taken as a personal affront by Bennett, who built the casino in a fit of vengeful spite. In reality, Bennett was not a member of the reading room and, bon vivant that he was, would not likely have suffered from the club's disapproval of his associates. In fact, the publisher had contacted architect Charles Follen McKim as early as February 1878 to discuss the project for the new social center he envisioned as the casino. Bennett also put his sister Jeannette and her husband, Isaac Bell, in touch with McKim for the construction of their own 1881–83 cottage three doors to the south of *Stone Villa*.

As publisher of the *New York Herald*, the newspaper founded by his father and boasting the highest daily circulation in America, and the *Paris Herald*, Bennett was responsible for the installation of the gatepost owls, emblematic of the *New York Herald* empire at the front gate of his Newport estate. From here, J. G. Bennett supervised the casino's activities, the yachting squadron, and the development of polo in America. Frustrated by his perception of the smugness of the American social elite, Bennett began to spend progressively more time in Europe; the house long associated with imperial Russia since Ambassador Middleton's day was leased by Bennett to successive Russian ambassadors as the summer legation and residence. In 1893, J. G. Bennett returned to his original idea of converting the property into resort use; plans were commissioned from the architect Whitney Warren for an elegant Queen Anne–Norman-style half-timbered hotel to wrap around *Stone Villa* and echo the casino in materials and design. Hesitancy by the cottage colony to frequent such a hotel may have derailed the project, which never advanced beyond the drawing stage. The estate's final owner was William Fitzhugh Whitehouse (1877–1955) of New York, from whose estate the property was acquired by developers in 1957 and demolished for the Bellevue Shopping Center.

Stone Villa, ca. 1955

Mrs. Paran Stevens Villa, ca. 1890

HOUSE N⁰· 22

PARAN STEVENS VILLA *(1866)*
Stevens Estate
George Platt, architect
Bellevue Avenue at Jones Street
Demolished

This lavish "steamboat Gothic" villa was built on a former Middleton lot behind *Stone Villa* for Mr. and Mrs. Paran Stevens of New York. Marietta Reed Stevens (1827–95) was the energetic and socially ambitious wife, and soon widow, of hotel entrepreneur Paran Stevens (1802–72), owner of the Fifth Avenue, Stevens House, and Victoria Hotels in New York and the Tremont in Boston. The Paran Stevenses first came to New-port in 1860 in the company of Marietta's younger sister, Fanny Reed (1834–1915), an aspiring singer whose rendition of the *Battle Hymn of the Republic* at the Bancroft cottage *Rosecliff* moved the hymn's authoress, Julia Ward Howe, to tears. With growing acclaim for her musical perfor-mances, Fanny moved to Europe, where she attracted the attention of the Prince of Wales, helping to assure the social ascension of her elder sister on both sides of the Atlantic. Entertaining at both 244 Fifth Avenue in New York and at Newport on a generous scale, the widowed Mrs. Stevens sought advantageous marriages for her two children, daughter Mary, or "Minnie" (1853–1919), and son Henry, "Harry" (1859–85). In 1876, Minnie served as a bridesmaid at the wedding of Newport friend Consuelo Yznaga to Lord Mandeville, heir to the Duke of Manchester, at Grace Episcopal Church in New York. This marriage had been closely preceded, in 1874, by the international wedding of Jennie Jerome, daughter of New York businessman Leonard Jerome, to Lord Randolph Churchill. In her pursuit of social recognition Mrs. Paran Stevens spent considerable time in England and France with Fanny publicizing the potential dowry of Minnie. By 1878, Minnie Stevens became the third of America's acknowledged "dollar princesses" when she wed Arthur Henry Fitzroy Paget, grandson of the first Marquis of Anglesey. As a sign of favor, Minnie, Lady Paget, received a private visit following the ceremony from the Prince of Wales offering his best wishes.

By 1880, Harry Leyden Stevens was also in love, with fellow Newport summer resident Edith Newbold Jones, daughter of George Frederic Jones and his wife, Lucretia, of *Pen Craig* cottage and great-niece of New York doyenne Mary Mason Jones. Such a promising alliance with the extended Jones-Newbold-Rhinelander family pleased Marietta Stevens,

Stevens Villa—Buckingham House hotel, ca. 1912

who announced the couple's engagement in the *Newport Daily News* of August 19, 1881. The Jones family appears to have had less enthusiastic thoughts; the engagement was called off by October. Mrs. Paran Stevens seems not to have lost her taste for young poets and literati, for the 1882 season witnessed her championing and hosting English poet and aesthete Oscar Wilde on the occasion of his July 15 lecture tour stop at the Newport Casino. In 1885, Edith N. Jones married Boston businessman Edward R. Wharton at Trinity Church chapel; Harry Stevens died, unmarried, a few months after the wedding at his mother's cottage. Edith Wharton sketched a satirical portrait of her erstwhile mother-in-law, Marietta Stevens, in *The Age of Innocence* where she appears as Mrs. Lemuel Struthers, the parvenue widow of a shoe polish magnate.

Lady Paget, soon a major London hostess, invited the divorced 8th Duke of Marlborough as a summer guest of her mother's in 1887, and the Duke embarked from the Stevens villa on his courtship of the wealthy American widow Lily Hamersley, later to become his duchess. At the rue de la Pompe, Paris, salon of Fanny Reed meanwhile, Mrs. Paran Stevens and her sister introduced heiress Anna Gould to Count Boniface de Castellane; "Boni" was invited to Newport to stay with Mrs. Stevens for the 1894 season. Acting as cotillion leader for Marietta, his tactic succeeded and the de Castellane–Gould union ensued. The strategy would be repeated by the 9th Duke of Marlborough, with Mrs. W. K. Vanderbilt of Marble House and Lady Paget serving, like her mother, as a marital agent in the 1895 engagement of the 9th Duke of Marlborough to Consuelo Vanderbilt (namesake of Consuelo Yznaga, Duchess of Manchester). Marietta Stevens died on April 3, 1895, in the former Mary Mason Jones mansion at 1 East Fifty-seventh Street and Fifth Avenue, long coveted but acquired only in 1893. The New York mansion was sold to Marietta Stevens' friend Theresa "Tessie" Fair Oelrichs of *Rosecliff*. The contents of the Newport villa were sold in July of 1895 and the villa itself was finally sold by the Stevens estate in March 1908 to a group of investors who converted it, fittingly, into a hotel known as the Buckingham House, wittily inspired by Lady Paget's London social aspirations. The hotel was demolished to extend the grounds and ensure the privacy of *Stone Villa* around 1925.

Lady Paget as Cleopatra, 1897,
Duke of Devonshire Ball, London

Arleigh, street facade, ca. 1910

HOUSE N⁰· 23

ARLEIGH *(1893)*
Mrs. H. Ruthven Pratt Estate
J. D. Johnston, architect
Bellevue Avenue at Parker Avenue
Demolished

Begun by Mrs. Mary Matthews in 1891 and completed by her daughter, Mrs. Harry Ruthven Pratt, the former Florence A. Matthews Singer (1859–1932), daughter of sewing machine inventor Isaac Merritt Singer, this Queen Anne–style villa, incorporating elements from the earlier cottage of Boston summer resident Harleston Parker (1823–88), was sublet as early as 1894 to Chicago dry goods merchant, developer, and hotelier Potter Palmer (1826–1902) and his wife, the former Bertha Matilde Honoré (1849–1918). Mrs. Palmer, an active contributor to artistic, civic, and women's affairs in Chicago, had achieved national celebrity from her role as chairman of the board of lady managers of the

1893 World's Columbian Exposition. In Newport, she was quickly taken up, and her Friday evening dinners and annual ball at *Arleigh* became highlights of the season. In 1897, Bertha Palmer inspected *Marble House* with Mrs. Alva Vanderbilt Belmont with an interest in buying the estate; Mrs. Belmont may have had a change of heart, for in 1898 the Potter Palmers went so far as to have plans drawn up for a villa of their own, which alas were never executed. The 1899 season found Mrs. Palmer busy arranging the Newport wedding of her niece Julia Dent Grant (1876–1975), granddaughter of President U. S. Grant, to Russian Prince Mikhail Cantacuzene. She rented the larger W. W. Astor estate *Beaulieu* to better accommodate the festivities preceding and following the September 24 ceremony. After the 1902 death of her husband, Bertha Palmer spent more time in Europe and Florida.

Arleigh was leased in 1903 to Isabel Gebhard Neilson of New York to host the wedding of her daughter Cathleen Neilson to Reginald C. Vanderbilt, and then in 1904 to Elizabeth Drexel Lehr (1868–1944) and her husband, society jester Henry "Harry" Symes Lehr (1869–1929), who would remain in residence for several years. On September 28, 1904, Harry Lehr and Mrs. Stuyvesant Fish gave a famous dog's dinner at *Arleigh* to celebrate the third birthday of Mrs. Lehr's Pomeranian, "Mighty Atom." Seven dog friends were invited with their mistresses. Atom, in a jeweled collar, sat at the head of a table set in the garden and decorated with dahlias, deep-red roses, and silver candelabra with deep-red fabric shades. The canine guests were seated in high chairs around the table with their mistresses directly behind them to assist the five butlers in serving a two-course menu of veal cutlets and frankfurters followed by ice cream, chocolates, and a birthday cake with three lighted candles. Dinner over, the guests were escorted to *Arleigh*'s drawing room, where Harry Lehr ushered in a few cats to rouse the lethargic guests. In 1907 the house was leased by Mr. and Mrs. James Ben Ali Haggin, who hosted receptions and musicales there until acquiring *Villa Rosa* in 1913. During the interwar years, the house was frequently unoccupied; ravaged by arson on June 13, 1932, *Arleigh* was torn down and a nursing home built on the long-vacant site in 1972.

Villa Rosa, garden facade, ca. 1904

HOUSE N⁰· 24

VILLA ROSA *(1901)*
Rollins Morse–Haggin Estate
Ogden Codman, architect
Bellevue Avenue between Dixon Street and Narragansett Avenue
Demolished

Built as the summer residence of Mr. Eben Rollins Morse (1845–1931), stockbroker of Boston, New York, and later Washington, D. C., and his wife, the former Marion Ronaldson Steedman (1849–1920), *Villa Rosa* was amongst Ogden Codman's (1853–1951) most successful American country houses. Three existing cottages were cleared for the site, north to south: the William F. & Elizabeth Coles cottage (1870, R. M. Hunt, architect for alterations), the Rebecca Jones cottage, and the Elizabeth S. Bryce cottage. Oriented to the south rather than east to the street, the house took maximum advantage of the resultant long, narrow setting. The gateposts led to a forecourt, followed by a walled inner court whose visual perspective from the street was terminated with a classical fountain set into a niche. The niche centered a trellis-decorated rear wing which was actually staff quarters, and the villa's neoclassical facade

Courtyard and entrance facade, ca. 1904

Entrance gate and forecourt, ca. 1930

Right: *Villa Rosa trellised ballroom (the allegorical bas-relief plaster panels seen set into the trelliswork were salvaged and were later in the collections of Belcourt Castle, Newport), ca. 1904*

Villa Rosa garden facade with the Haggin grandchildren, ca. 1915.

opened to the left onto the gravel courtyard. This plan was based on that of eighteenth-century French aristocratic townhouses and was unique in America in 1900. The exterior of the house was covered in pastel yellow stucco, later painted pink, offset with white bas-relief panels, and was crowned by a copper dome. The lawn terminated at Narragansett Avenue with a circular marble gazebo copied from Marie Antoinette's Temple of Love (1778) by Richard Mique at Versailles.

Villa Rosa's interiors were equally impressive. A rigorous French classicism dominated, with off-white or white-and-green paneled reception rooms. The heart of the house was the green-trellised circular music room or ballroom, the first room in the United States to incorporate lattice design as a comprehensive decorative scheme. The Morses appear to have been pleased, for in 1905 they commissioned Codman to design and decorate a similarly neoclassical townhouse built at 7 East Fifty-first Street in New York, where the couple had moved in 1902.

In 1913, *Villa Rosa* was leased to and then purchased, for a reported $350,000, by James Ben Ali Haggin (1822–1913), a wealthy mining operator and turfman of Nob Hill, San Francisco; Lexington, Kentucky; and 1 East Sixty-fourth Street, New York. The widowed Haggin had remarried in 1897; Margaret Sanders Voorhies Haggin (1869–1965) was the niece of his first wife, Eliza Sanders, and known as one of the most beautiful women in Kentucky. Together they took up New York society life with enthusiasm. Sadly, Mr. Haggin died at Newport on September 13, 1914. *Villa Rosa* was sold by the estate of its final occupant, Mrs. Emily Coddington Williams (1876–1952), Rhode Island novelist and author, on July 20, 1953, for $21,500 to E. A. McNulty, a Rhode Island contractor. Ogden Codman's masterpiece was demolished in December of 1962 and a brick apartment complex (now condominiums) built on the site in 1965. Townhouse condominiums replaced the gardens in 1980 and the gateposts, one of the final vestiges, were cleared in 2004.

Mrs. James Haggin, ca. 1915

Villa Rosa, entrance hall, ca. 1904

Villa Rosa, drawing room, ca. 1905

Villa Rosa, dining room, ca. 1904

Villa Rosa, dining room, ca. 1904

Villa Rosa, rose garden arbor and south facade, ca. 1905

Villa Rosa, ca. 1955

G. H. Warren House, west facade, ca. 1900

HOUSE N°· 25

ROBERT RAY–G. H. WARREN HOUSE *(CA. 1852)*
Ray-Warren Estate
George Champlin Mason & Son, architects (renovation)
Clay Street
Demolished

Erected as a summer cottage in the early 1850s for a pioneering New York summer colonist, the merchant Robert Ray (1794–1879), the house pre-dated Newport promoter and architect George Champlin Mason Sr.'s 1860 development of a cottage row along the north side of the Narragansett Avenue corridor with Mason-designed summer homes for such prominent New York summer colonists as the Ogden, Schermerhorn, and Tiffany families. The Robert Ray house was entered via a semicircular drive facing west off Clay Street. Facing south toward Narragansett Avenue, a projecting wing with a single-story bay window was joined by a wraparound, arched veranda to a flanking wing with an asymmetrical candle-snuffer-topped turret. The narrower three-bay main entrance facade faced Clay Street and was dominated by a stepped fieldstone and brick-capped chimney.

In 1881, the property was acquired by New York lawyer and financier George Henry Warren (1823–92), a founder of the Metropolitan Opera House, his wife, the former Mary Caroline Phoenix (1832-1901), and the seven surviving of their ten children. Renovations were undertaken by Mason and his son, George Champlin Mason Jr. A cherry-paneled center hall was created, leading to a richly adorned Renaissance Revival dining room. Of the Warren family group, architect son Lloyd Elliot Warren (1868–1922) would remain at his parents' house; eldest daughter, Harriette Louise Warren (1854–1912) would marry Robert Goelet and reside at their nearby Narragansett Avenue villa *Ochre Point* (McKim, Mead & White,1882); eldest son George Henry Warren II (1855–1943), lawyer and stockbroker, and his wife, Georgia Williams, would acquire *Seafield* on Ocean Avenue at the close of the nineteenth century; younger brother, Beaux-Arts–trained architect Whitney Warren (1864–1943) and wife, Charlotte A. Tooker, purchased the former Harper cottage directly behind his father's house; and sister Edith Caroline Warren (1866–1944) married William Starr Miller and erected first *Maplehurst* (McKim, Mead & White, 1883) nearby on Bellevue Avenue and later *High Tide* (1903) with her brother Whitney Warren. The George H. Warren cottage was sold by the family on September 20, 1921, to their neighbor to the east, Emily Morris (Mrs. R. Horace) Gallatin. Mrs. Gallatin promptly demolished the house to incorporate the site into the grounds of her property, *Chepstow.*

George H. Warren House, south facade, ca. 1920

Whitney Warren House, ca. 1920

HOUSE Nº· 26

WHITNEY WARREN HOUSE *(CA. 1860)*
Harper-Warren Estate
Attributed to George Champlin Mason, architect
Clay Street at Parker Avenue
Demolished

By 1885, George H. Warren's son, the budding architect Whitney Warren (1864–1943), had acquired the virtually neighboring Emily Louisa
Harper Pennington cottage for himself and his new bride, Charlotte
Tooker (1864–1951) of Newport and New York, creating a kind of family compound.

Built circa 1860, probably by local architect G. C. Mason, the cottage
was originally the summer residence of Emily Louisa Harper (1835–

1908), the only surviving child of three born to Charles Carroll Harper (1802–37) of Baltimore, grandson and namesake of Charles Carroll of Carrollton, and his wife, Charlotte Cheffelle Harper. Charles C. Harper's mother, Catharine Carroll Harper (Mrs. Robert Godloe Harper), and unmarried sister, Emily Louisa Harper, his daughter's godmother, had been summering in Newport since the 1830s; it is likely that the widowed grandmother and unmarried aunt invited Emily to join them in Newport following Emily's father's death and her own 1853 marriage to Baltimore lawyer William Clapham Pennington. After residing in the Harper's Ocean Avenue cottage, the Penningtons decided to build their own residence following the birth of their two sons, Robert G. Harper Pennington and Clapham Pennington. The lot was one of several Mrs. Catharine Carroll Harper had purchased in the vicinity of Narragansett and Bellevue Avenues on arriving in Newport, and the specific location may have been inspired by the marriage of cousin John Lee Carroll (1830–1911) to Anita Phelps (1838–73), daughter of Royal Phelps of New York, who lived directly opposite on Clay Street.

Charlotte Tooker, the future Mrs. Whitney Warren, was raised with her parents, Mr. and Mrs. Gabriel M. Tooker, at the corner of Kay Street and Bellevue Avenue, facing the home of Richard Morris Hunt, prior to her July 13, 1884, wedding to Whitney Warren. The young Warren's career would blossom in Newport with his winning the 1894 competition to design the Newport County Club, only a year after returning from the Ecole des Beaux-Arts. He would go on to design the Grand Central Terminal, the New York Yacht Club, and numerous hotels. Whitney and Charlotte Warren had three children: Charlotte A. Warren (1885–1957), Mrs. William Greenough; Gabrielle Warren (1895–1971), Mrs. Reginald B. Rives; and Whitney Warren Jr. (1898–1986). Whitney Warren's estate would subsequently sell the property in 1943 to Newport real estate investor Eugene J. O'Reilly, who converted the house into apartments. Preferring not to see the family home used in this manner, the heirs of Whitney Warren repurchased the property in 1955 and had the house demolished for residential subdivision.

Whiteholme, garden facade, ca. 1930

HOUSE N⁰. 27

WHITEHOLME *(1901)*
Mrs. Robert Garrett Estate
John Russell Pope, architect
Narragansett Avenue at Ochre Point Avenue
Demolished

For the large family of popular New York attorney and Wall Street investor William R. Travers (1819–87), the architect Richard Morris Hunt worked between 1869 and 1872 to add reception and family rooms to his renovation of the 1862 Thomas H. Hitchcock Stick Style villa on the south side of Narragansett Avenue. Travers, a famous patron of horse racing, is best remembered as a partner of Leonard Jerome and as the father of Matilda Travers Gay (1856–1943), devoted wife of the painter Walter Gay (1856–1937).

Following Travers' death, the property was acquired as the summer villa

Whiteholme, salon, ca. 1905

of Mary Frick Garrett (1851–1936) and her husband, Robert Garrett (1847–96), retired president of the Baltimore and Ohio Railroad. The Garretts had, in 1887, just completed renovations to adjoining brownstones on Mount Vernon Square in Baltimore with the architects McKim, Mead & White and thus lived within the confines of the Travers villa until Mr. Garrett's declining mental health might improve; it further declined and Garrett died in 1896. Mrs. Garrett decided to rebuild shortly thereafter, and *Whiteholme,* as she was to call the new residence, had the distinction of being among the first commissions of the celebrated neoclassic architect John Russell Pope (1873–1938). Pope had graduated from the Ecole des Beaux Arts in 1900 and was still working in the New York architectural office of Bruce Price when selected by Mrs. Garrett; the suggestion likely came from her future husband, Dr. Henry Barton Jacobs (1858–1939), her late husband's physician, who knew Pope's uncle from their days at Harvard. Mary Garrett teamed the young architect with the Paris decorator Jules Allard, who had worked on the interiors of the Garrett townhouse on Mount Vernon Square in Baltimore. The resulting "modern French" classical villa was a success, and Mary Garrett

Whiteholme, west wing, ca. 1905

Jacobs hired Pope to enlarge her Baltimore townhouse in 1905 with new French reception rooms. She also introduced the architect to Baltimore railroad magnate Henry Walters (1848–1931). From this contact, the Baltimore Museum of Art would later result, as would an introduction by Walters to railroad investor Pembroke Jones (1858–1919) and his wife, the former Sarah Wharton Green (1859–1943). Walters lived with the Pembroke Joneses in *Sherwood* at Newport, *Airlie* in Wilmington, North Carolina, and at 5 East Sixty-first Street in New York. In 1912, John Russell Pope married the very social Jones' daughter Sadie (1887–1975), an event which brought him into direct contact with a host of potential patrons. Following the 1919 death of Pembroke Jones, Sarah married Henry Walters, whose friendship with the Delano family brought Pope to the attention of Franklin Delano Roosevelt, who shared the architect's classical vision for American public architecture. In Newport, Pope was, at an early stage, busy on renovations to *Belcourt*, *Chetwode*, the Redwood Library, and new construction including Tudor Revival *Bonniecrest* (1918) for the Stuart Duncans and the Popes' own organic Tudor-esque villa and studio *The Waves*, completed in 1927 on the site of the looming *Lippitt's Castle*.

At Mrs. Garrett's *Whiteholme*, the existing Hitchcock-Travers House was encased in stucco; Pope grafted to its front an unusual Y-shaped glazed stucco-over-brick structure opening to a tree-lined *allée* leading to the intersection of Narragansett and Ochre Point Avenues. The unusual Y shape design, of which the stem of the letter was the old Travers house, may have been influenced by Whitney Warren's 1894 plan for the Newport Country Club. The urbane French interiors were in Louis XV and Louis XVI taste, and the statuary-filled garden was noted for its compact formality. Following Dr. Henry Barton Jacobs' death, *Whiteholme* was sold in 1940 to real estate investor James C. O'Donnell, of Washington and Newport, for $20,000, and shortly thereafter resold by him in 1944 for $26,000 to its final private occupant, author and poet Annette Townsend Phillips (1885–1965) of Newport. Subsequently purchased by Thomas P. Bilodeau, the estate was acquired by Salve Regina College on January 8, 1963, and was demolished in April 1963 for the construction of Miley Hall, a modern student residence and dining facility. Donald Tinney (1934–2006) of Newport acquired the painted and natural carved-wood paneling from several reception rooms for the collection at *Belcourt Castle*, and a pair of allegorical statues from the garden were acquired by a Kansas City developer, J. C. Nichols, and moved to Prairie Village, Kansas.

Above: Whiteholme, entrance facade, ca. 1945
Right: Whiteholme, gates, ca. 1905

Whiteholme, garden facade, ca. 1905

Sulthorne, ca. 1970

HOUSE N⁰· 28

SULTHORNE *(1847)*
Lyman Estate
Seth C. Bradford, architect
Webster Street between Bellevue and Lawrence Avenues
Demolished

After summering in local boarding-houses since the late 1830s, Mrs. Charles Lyman, the former Susan Powell Warren (1806–56) of Beacon Hill, Boston, hired Newport builder-architect Seth Bradford (1801–78) to erect a large white timber-framed Gothic Revival cottage. The commission was one of Bradford's first and its success may have attracted the interest of William Shepard Wetmore, who would engage Bradford to build his granite Italianate villa *Château-sur-Mer* in 1851. The house was inherited by her son Charles Frederick

From the Gustave J. S. White auction catalog, July 1973

Lyman and his wife, Annie Mason Grant Lyman, and daughter, Florence Lyman; they in turn passed the estate on to Charles' daughter Annie Lyman (1878–1954), who left it to her husband Cyril B. Judge (1890–1973), president of the Newport Country Club. With the 1973 death of Cyril B. Judge, the contents were auctioned and the property sold to Elinor Dorrance Hill Ingersoll (1907–77), owner of an adjacent estate. The house was demolished that year and the grounds used as open space by Mrs. Ingersoll. The property has since been sold by her heirs and is now subdivided for luxury homes; slightly over one acre, however, was preserved as open space with conservation easements in 2009.

Graystone, gates, ca. 1890

HOUSE N⁰· 29

GRAYSTONE *(1883)*
Bosworth-Wysong-Jelke Estate
George Champlin Mason, architect
Ochre Point Avenue between Victoria and Ruggles Avenues
Demolished

The aptly named *Graystone* was a rough-hewn Fall River granite Romanesque Revival villa built for Fitch J. Bosworth (1826–85), heir to
Milwaukee wholesale druggists H. Bosworth & Sons, in 1883 by local architects George Champlin Mason & Son. Following Bosworth's
1885 death, the house was sold in 1887 to New York socialites James
J. Wysong (1839–1910) and his wife, the former Martha Marshall (d.
1925), heir, with her sister Louise, to the fortune of dry goods merchant John Rutgers Marshall. In New York, the J. J. Wysongs moved from
30 East Thirty-fourth Street to a new mansion at 1 East Seventy-sixth
Street by architect and Newport summer resident F. L. V. Hoppin of
Hoppin & Koen in 1910.

Graystone, north facade, ca. 1890

Graystone, south facade, ca. 1890

The interiors of *Graystone* were noted for a stained glass program designed by Donald MacDonald for William McPherson & Co. of Boston, and the house was significantly renovated by Newport architect J. D. Johnston in 1889. The estate was last owned by the Jelke family when purchased from Martha M. Wysong's estate in 1925 by Ferdinand Frazier Jelke (1888–1953) for the use of his father. F. Frazier Jelke had, in 1924, built *Eagle's Nest* on Ocean Avenue with William Aldrich and Henry Sleeper. Jelke's father, Chicago oleo-margarine manufacturer John Faris Jelke (1856–1931), and his wife, Louanna Frazier Jelke (1859–1932), took up residency in *Graystone*. The estate was later inherited by F. Frazier Jelke's elder brother, John F. Jelke Jr. (1887–1965), and was destroyed by a fire of undetermined origin during the evening of May 31, 1938. The gateposts and boundary wall survive, but the site is now the visitor parking lot of *The Breakers*, directly opposite.

Graystone, ca. 1910

Graystone, ca. 1895

The Cloisters, gates, ca. 1930

HOUSE N⁰· 30

THE CLOISTERS *(1887)*
Kernochan-Woodward Estate
John Dixon Johnston, architect; alterations by Delano & Aldrich
Ruggles Avenue at Wetmore Avenue
Demolished

The Cloisters, facing Wetmore Avenue and backing up to Taylor's Beach and the Cliff Walk, was built as a timber-framed and granite-faced guest cottage with a large round-arched granite column veranda that gave the house its name. Originally the property of Catherine Lorillard Kernochan (1835–1917), whose circa 1870 villa by G. C. Mason, *Seaview*, stood next door to the west, the house was one of several in the immediate vicinity erected by the children and relatives of tobacco heir Pierre III (1796–1867) and Catherine Griswold Lorillard. Brother Pierre IV built

The Cloisters, garden facade, ca. 1930

The Cloisters, from Cliff Walk, ca. 1890

The Breakers in 1878 with architects Peabody & Stearns, which he subsequently sold in 1885 to Cornelius Vanderbilt II prior to establishing
the community of Tuxedo Park, New York. Cousin Catherine Lorillard
Wolfe built *Vinland* also with Peabody & Stearns in 1883 immediately to
the north. Catherine married James Powell Kernochan (1831–97), son
of a wealthy Louisiana sugar plantation owner, and resided with him and
her two children, Catherine Lorillard Kernochan Pell (1858–1917) and
James Lorillard Kernochan (1868–1903), in Newport and at 824 Fifth
Avenue, where her husband died from injuries suffered when struck by
a carriage. Withdrawing to Newport, Catherine L. Kernochan began
divesting herself of property, leasing the New York townhouse and sell-
ing *The Cloisters* by 1900 to New York financier and chairman of the
Hanover National Bank of New York James T. Woodward (1837–1910).

The Cloisters, street facade, ca. 1930

James Thomas Woodward, of 9 East Fifty-sixth Street, New York, had acquired real estate in Newport by 1893, but his primary focus was to be racing and breeding thoroughbreds at his country estate and stud farm *Belair* near Bowie, Maryland, purchased in 1898. J. T. Woodward never married, and his *Belair* and *The Cloisters* were left to his nephew William C. Woodward (1876–1953), who also took over the chairmanship of Hanover National Bank.

William and his wife, Elizabeth "Elsie" Cryder Woodward (1882–1981), embarked on major renovation campaigns with the architectural firm of Delano & Aldrich, at *Belair* in 1913–14 and at *The Cloisters* in 1914–15, followed by the construction of a limestone-clad neo-Georgian town-house at 9 East Eighty-sixth Street in 1916–18 with the same firm. Both William and Elsie Woodward had long-established Rhode Island ties: William's mother was the former Sarah Rodman of South Kingstown; and Elsie's mother was the former Elizabeth Callendar Ogden of Newport; her father, Duncan Cryder, was the nephew of William Shepard Wetmore of nearby *Château-sur-Mer*, Newport. The Woodwards' renovated Queen Anne–Shingle Style house on Wetmore Avenue was demolished in 1950 and the site later subdivided for contemporary homes. The stucco-encased Kernochan stable survives as a residence fronting on Ruggles Avenue.

Mayfield, entrance facade, 1914

HOUSE N⁰· 31

MAYFIELD *(CA. 1865)*
Tiffany-Kane-Camoys-Drexel Estate
Bellevue Avenue at Gordon Street
Demolished

At the core of *Mayfield* was a rural circa 1793 farmhouse traditionally thought to have belonged to the Coggeshall family and forming the northern wing of the subsequent structure. Used as a summer rental cottage, the property was acquired in the early 1850s by Henry Tiffany (1811–77) and his wife, Sally Jones McLane Tiffany (1820–87), of Baltimore. Tiffany, brother of George Tiffany residing on nearby Narragansett Avenue, commissioned alterations from a local builder, N. Barker, around 1865, followed by additions by Newport resident architect George Champlin Mason in 1866. The succeeding owner was Walter Langdon Kane (1843–96), son of Newport–New York sportsman Oliver DeLancey Kane and his wife, Louisa Astor Langdon Kane, of *Beach Cliffe*. Kane undertook further alterations around 1880 with local architect Dudley Newton; this campaign moved the house back on its lot and gave the exterior its Stick Style exposed decorative beams, Queen Anne detailing, and altered roofline. Walter Kane's wife was Mary Rotch Hunter (1854–1936), daughter of Charles and Mary Rotch Hunter, who perished on the wreck of the *Ville du Havre*. Following Kane's 1896 death, Mary married an Englishman, the Honourable William Edward Glyn (1859–1939), who christened the house *Mayfield*. In 1946 Mildred Constance Sherman Stonor (1888–1961), daughter of banker William Watts Sherman and Sophia Augusta Brown Sherman of the Watts-Sherman house, Newport, purchased the property. Mildred Sherman had married the Honourable Ralph Julian Stonor (1884–1968), 5th Lord Camoys, and chose to return to Newport after World War II, renaming *Mayfield* as *Stonor Lodge* in honor of her husband's Oxfordshire family seat. Lady Camoys, in turn, left the property to her daughter, the Honourable Noreen Stonor Drexel (1922–2012), wife of John R. Drexel III (1919–2007). As an active philanthropist and preservationist, Mrs. Drexel made *Stonor Lodge* a hub of civic and social dialogue. Sold out of the family following her death, the house was undergoing sympathetic restoration when consumed by a fast-moving fire on February 25, 2016.

d'Hauteville Cottage, ca. 1875

HOUSE N⁰· 32

D'HAUTEVILLE COTTAGE *(1871)*
d'Hauteville-Drury Estate
Peabody & Stearns, architects
Bellevue Avenue between Gordon Street and Victoria Avenue
Demolished

A fanciful half-timbered Stick Style cottage, this house was one of the first residential commissions of the architectural firm of Peabody & Stearns, designed for Frederick Sears Grand d'Hauteville (1838–1918) of Boston. Frederick was the son of Boston heiress Ellen Sears (1819–62) and a Swiss father, Paul Gonzalve Grand d'Hauteville of the château d'Hauteville near Vevey, Switzerland. The couple had met while Ellen was touring Europe and married in 1837; within a year the homesick and pregnant Ellen Sears d'Hauteville left her husband and returned to her parents, Senator David Sears (1787–1871) and Miriam Clark Sears, at 42 Beacon Street (now the Somerset Club). A child, Frederick, was born in Boston, and when Ellen refused to return to Switzerland and surrender custody of her son, a widely publicized lawsuit ensued between Paul d'Hauteville and the Sears family. Known as the d'Hauteville case, it challenged the common law paternalistic practice of fathers making decisions regarding custody. The case was settled only in 1840 in Ellen Sears' favor and resulted in legislation, sponsored by the influential Sears family and passing in Rhode Island in 1841, curtailing the custody rights of foreign husbands. The d'Hautevilles divorced in 1841 and he remarried the following year Catherine von Zeppelin. Ellen raised her son on Beacon Street and at the David Sears summer residence *Red Cross*, an 1844 Gothic Revival cottage by architect George Minot Dexter on Oakwood Terrace in Newport.

After service in the Civil War, young Frederick married Elizabeth Stuyvesant Fish, daughter of Hamilton Fish of New York. Following her premature death in 1864, he married Susan Watts Macomb (1849–1928), granddaughter of War of 1812 hero General Alexander Macomb, in 1872 and had three children. The cottage was acquired from the d'Hauteville estate in 1929 by Francis Saxham Elwes Drury (1859–1937) of London, who had, in 1925, married Mabel Gerry (1872–1931) of Newport and New York. Mabel was the daughter of Elbridge Thomas Gerry (1837–1927), prominent New York attorney, and his wife, Louisa Matilda Livingston (1836–1920) of *Seaverge* on lower Bellevue Avenue. Rebaptized *Drury Lodge*, the house remained in the family into the 1950s, when, following a fire, it was largely razed. A truncated fragment of the house remains.

d'Hauteville Cottage—Drury Lodge, ca. 1948

Stoneacre, street facade, ca. 1930

HOUSE №· 33

STONEACRE *(1882)*
Ellis-Loew Estate
William Appleton Potter, architect
Bellevue Avenue between Victoria and Ruggles Avenues
Demolished

This vast Shingle Style cottage, with a broad front piazza and exotic dome overlooking grounds designed by Frederick Law Olmsted, was built for John W. Ellis (1817–1910), founder of the First National Bank in Cincinnati and a director of the Northern Pacific Railroad. Sold to E. R. and Linda Thomas, the estate was then acquired in 1916 and renovated by Manhattan stockbroker William Goadby Loew (1876–1955) and his wife, the former Florence Baker (1876–1936) of New York. Mrs. Loew was the daughter of financier George Fisher Baker (1840–1931) and with her family trust erected a large English Regency–style townhouse at 56 East Ninety-third Street with architects Walker & Gillette in 1931. Her brother George F. Baker Jr. had, in 1927, bought the former Francis Palmer house (1918) by Delano & Aldrich at the corner of Ninety-third and Fifth and had the same architects expand the residence down Ninety-third Street.

Following a fire in 1953, the Loew family sold *Stoneacre* in 1955 to Gustave Pierre Bader for $24,500. Bader transferred ownership to the Hatch Preparatory School in 1957, and the property became, with a half-dozen estates along central Bellevue Avenue, a dormitory first for the Hatch School and later for Vernon Court Junior College. Demolished in 1962 for a planned academic building and recreational campus, these new construction plans were canceled by the 1973 bankruptcy of the school. While the other former estate dormitories were developed into condominiums, the site of *Stoneacre* remained empty and is now preserved as the Frederick Law Olmsted Park. The surviving stable building was saved by conversion into condominiums in 1986 and is now a student residence for Salve Regina University.

Stoneacre, ca. 1950
Left: *Stoneacre, ca. 1888*

Pansy Cottage—Chetwode stables, ca. 1900

Storrs Wells—Pansy Cottage, ca. 1898

Chetwode, garden facade, ca. 1910

HOUSE N⁰· 34

CHETWODE *(1903)*
Storrs Wells–Astor-Andrews Estate
Horace Trumbauer, architect
Bellevue Avenue between Victoria and Ruggles Avenues
Demolished

In 1890, William Storrs Wells (1849–1926) of New York, director and president of the Fairbanks Company, manufacturer of scales, and his wife, Anna "Annie" Cole Raynor Wells (1854–1935), daughter of James A. Raynor, president of the Erie Railroad, acquired *Pansy Cottage* at the western corner of Bellevue and Ruggles Avenues. The cottage had been built as a rental property, probably by G. C. Mason for J. N. A. Griswold of Newport circa 1865, and was later sold to Constant Abrams Andrews (1844–1919), son of Loring Andrews, whose vertiginous Stick Style villa (1872) stood nearby. C. A. Andrews engaged Richard Morris Hunt to remodel in 1870–71. To the north of *Pansy Cottage*, sharing the block, were the Henry Sigourney and Adele Clapp houses, which Wells acquired and removed in the ensuing decade. By 1900, a long timber-framed addition on the newly cleared Bellevue frontage was completed to the plans of architect W. Tyson Gooch; the new wing contained a French salon, dining room, and morning room together with new master bedrooms, all designed and executed by decorator Jules Allard of Paris and New York. A Tudor Revival stucco and half-timbered stable was erected by the young Philadelphia architect Horace Trumbauer at the back of the lot. On May 4, 1900, just as the Storrs Wellses were about to set out for Newport, *Pansy Cottage* was completely destroyed by fire.

Undeterred, William and Annie Storrs Wells set out to rebuild on a grander scale. Siting the new masonry house of Roman brick trimmed with limestone on the footprint of the original, at an angle to the intersection, the Wellses hired Trumbauer to work with Allard. The approved model was inspired by the 1765 château de Montmusard near Dijon with a garden facade organized around a central rotunda, preceded by

Chetwode, hall chimneypiece, ca. 1910

a peristyle and flanked by two wings. With formal landscaping by the architect John Russell Pope and opulent interior reception rooms by Allard, *Chetwode*, as the new villa was named, became one of the most lavish homes ever erected in Newport. The white-and-gold paneled salons were in Louis XV and Louis XVI taste based on the king's private apartments at Versailles. The dining room, library, and morning room contained Old Master paintings set into the wall decoration. Following her husband's death Mrs. Wells generally occupied the summer home until the 1930 season; the estate was then leased to A. J. Drexel Biddle Jr. for three years and then sold, largely furnished, on January 23, 1934, to John Jacob Astor V (1912–96) for $150,000. The estate then comprised a garage-stable block, gardener's cottage, greenhouse, five acres of formal

Chetwode, dining room, ca. 1930

Chetwode, grand salon, ca. 1930

gardens, and grounds extending beyond Coggeshall Avenue west to Carroll Avenue. Astor was born four months after his father, Colonel John Jacob Astor IV (1864–1912), died in the sinking of the *Titanic*; his pregnant mother, Madeleine Force Astor (1893–1940), was rescued and raised her son in New York and in Newport at the family estate, *Beechwood*. The twenty-one-year-old Astor heir had just come of age and was engaged to marry Miss Eileen Sherman Gillespie of Newport in February 1934. When that wedding was called off, J. J. Astor courted her Newport friend Ellen Tuck French (1915–74), daughter of Francis O. French of New York and *Harbourview*, Newport. They were married June 30, 1934, at Trinity Church and set up seasonal residency at *Chetwode*, soon joined by their baby son William B. Astor (1935–2008). Newlywed Doris Duke Cromwell sublet the estate from the Astors for the 1937 season. The marriage ended in divorce in 1943, and the following year Astor married Gertrude Gretsch, with whom he had a daughter, Jacqueline.

In 1948, the J. J. Astors placed the estate and contents on the auction block. Numerous pieces acquired at that sale are now in the collections of *Rosecliff* and *Rough Point*. The property sold in October of 1948 for $71,000 to James C. O'Donnell, a chain drugstore owner and real estate investor. His daughter, Mrs. Florence O'Donnell Maher, sold the estate

Chetwode, ca. 1938

to the Texas-based Church of Christ for $45,000 in 1954, for use as a church and center for servicemen. In June of 1957, the church sold *Chetwode* for $40,000 to Thomas Diab and John P. Curran, Boston developers, for conversion into apartments. Finally, in November of 1958 the estate was sold, again for $40,000, to Miss Phoebe Warren Andrews (1909–75) of New York, who, as president of the Newport Art League, held exhibitions and sponsored a residential art school in the house. She similarly operated residences for young people in the arts at Beaux-Arts townhouses acquired at Sixty-eighth and Fifth and 35 East Sixty-eighth Street in New York. During the morning of January 29, 1972, a chimney fire spread through the three floors of the villa, causing devastating damage. Although retrievable, the house was not restored for lack of funds and its intact interiors were sold off. The French paneling and mantels of the reception rooms are known to have been salvaged by the Tinney family and others, and are today dispersed between shops, restaurants, and private collections in Newport, Boston, New Jersey, and Paris. *Chetwode*, one of the chief glories of Newport, was razed in May of 1973. The outlying acreage from Ruggles to Carroll Avenues had become, after 1948, the setting for multiple residential subdivisions. The remaining five acres of gardens sold in August of 1976 for $96,000 for development into a six-lot subdivision, and the surviving 1900 stable-garage building was converted into condominiums.

Chetwode, garden fountain, ca. 1910

Top: *Chetwode, library, ca. 1930*
Bottom: *Chetwode, hall, ca. 1930*

Top: *Chetwode, petit salon, ca. 1930*
Middle: *Chetwode, red drawing room, ca. 1930*
Bottom: *Chetwode, aerial view, ca. 1935*

Mrs. August Belmont,
ca. 1870

Mrs. Belmont in her demi d'Aumont *carriage, ca. 1870*

By-the-Sea, ca. 1875

HOUSE N⁰· 35

BY-THE-SEA *(1860)*
Belmont-McLean Estate
George Champlin Mason Sr., architect; alterations by Horace Trumbauer
Bellevue Avenue at Marine Avenue
Demolished

Due to family ties that united the Perry and Champlin families in New-port, George Champlin Mason's (1820–94) fledgling architectural prac-tice was assured when launched in 1860 with the commission for the August Belmont villa, *By-the-Sea.* Belmont (1813–90), New York finan-cier and horse breeder, had just purchased fourteen acres of oceanfront land on southern Bellevue Avenue for $47,000. Mason's commission was received through Mrs. Belmont, née Caroline Perry (1829–92), a daughter of Commodore Matthew Calbraith Perry (1794–1858) of Newport. Mr. Belmont began his own career in New York by founding, as the Rothschild family's American representative, the firm of August Belmont & Co., handling foreign exchange, loans, and corporate trans-actions following the 1837 Panic; he subsequently became involved in politics as a diplomat and chairman of the Democratic National Com-

Top: *By-the-Sea, Cliff Walk façade, ca. 1910*
Bottom: *By-the-Sea, salon, ca. 1910*

mittee. Choosing to abandon a country seat on Staten Island to summer in her native Newport with her husband, four sons, and one daughter, Mrs. Belmont led the march of elegant New York society to Newport and introduced a Rothschild penchant for things French to the summer colony, from liveried footmen, elaborate entertainments, and fashionable costumes to a celebrated *demi d'Aumont* carriage model.

The new house was formulaic early Mason: an Italianate timber-framed cottage with low-hipped mansard roof, a three-bay entrance front pavilion, and conventional bracketed trim. *By-the-Sea* was updated considerably with classicizing alterations undertaken by Horace Trumbauer in 1910 for the Belmont's eldest son, Perry Belmont (1851–1947), banker and four-term congressman of Washington, D.C. Trumbauer had just completed Perry's Washington residence on Connecticut Avenue, now the headquarters of the Order of the Eastern Star. Brother Oliver Hazard Perry Belmont (1858–1908) had built his own Richard Morris Hunt–designed villa, *Belcourt* (1894), farther south on Bellevue in 1892 and welcomed his second wife, Alva Smith Vanderbilt, of *Marble House* there in 1896.

Owned by Perry Belmont, *By-the-Sea* became a rental property when he was not in residence and was leased for decades to the legendary Washington-based socialite Evalyn Walsh MacLean (1886–1947), who had been summering in Newport since her childhood, a childhood marred early on by tragedy that would frequently haunt her life. Evalyn and her younger brother Vinson (1888–1905), only children of millionaire gold miner Thomas Walsh (1850–1910), were driving to a luncheon at the Clambake Club outside Newport when the roadster Vinson was driving hit a bridge railing and the car overturned into a ditch, leaving the young driver with fatal head injuries. Evalyn's own son, Vinson, would later die in a car accident, and her husband, Edward McLean, heir to the *Washington Post*, suffer a mental collapse. Many saw in this the supposed curse of the Hope diamond, which Ned McLean had given Evalyn in 1911; she would be its final private owner.

By-the-Sea, garden facade, ca. 1930

The property was subsequently sold for delinquent taxes from the 44 East 34th Street Corporation to James C. O'Donnell, who promptly re-sold to Ray Alan Van Clief (1892–1947), the then owner of *Rosecliff*, the abutting former Theresa Fair Oelrichs estate. Mr. Van Clief demolished *By-the-Sea* in 1946 to join its lands with those of *Rosecliff*. Following Van Clief's sudden death, the Belmont and Oelrichs estates were jointly sold in 1947 to J. Edgar Monroe of New Orleans, who in 1971 donated the combined properties to the Preservation Society. Twelve acres, comprising the bulk of the fourteen acres of the former *By-the-Sea* property, were soon thereafter sold to a land investment company and proceeds placed in an endowment for *Rosecliff*. The estate grounds were subdivided and modern homes built on the site beginning in 1986.

W. W. Tucker House, ca. 1875

HOUSE N°. 36

W. W. TUCKER HOUSE *(1869)*
Tucker-Post Estate
George Champlin Mason, architect; alterations by J. D. Johnston
Bellevue Avenue facing Marine Avenue
Demolished

Bostonian William W. Tucker (1817–85) of Upham, Tucker & Co. commission merchants, and his wife, Susan Elizabeth Lawrence Tucker of 98 Beacon Street, engaged Newport architect George Champlin Mason to build their Italianate cottage near the cliffs at the southern-most end of Bellevue Avenue overlooking a chasm that inspired the estate's original name, *The Grotto.* The views from this cottage appealed to the Vanderbilt brothers. From 1881 until his purchase of the former Lorillard estate in 1885, Cornelius Vanderbilt II (1843–99) sublet the Tucker cottage every season. His younger brother, Frederick W. Vanderbilt (1856–1938), subsequently acquired the Tucker property and began construction on the site of the more palatial *Rough Point* in 1888. He had the timber-framed Tucker house moved to a new site north on Bellevue Avenue and renovated by J. D. Johnston. The cottage was then presented to the Post family, Mrs. William Post, the former Rosalie DeWolf Anthony (1844–1929), being a sister of Mrs. Frederick W. Vanderbilt, née Louise Anthony (1844–1926). The house in turn passed to Margaret Louise "Daisy" Post (1876–1969), the future Mrs. James L. Van Alen and later still Mrs. Louis Bruguière. Daisy Post, born in Newport, spent summers here as a girl and winters at her uncle Frederick Vanderbilt's estate at Hyde Park, New York; she would subsequently become his primary heir. Rebaptized *Rosetta Villa* by the Posts, the house was sold by Mrs. Bruguière to Newport real estate developer James T. O'Connell (1889–1974), who razed the villa in 1938. The site was part of the Vernon Court Junior College complex between 1964 and 1971 and was later sold as a vacant residential lot in 2004. A sizable new French manor house now occupies the site.

Hawthorne Villa, ca. 1910

HOUSE N^{O.} 37

HAWTHORNE VILLA *(1860)*
Smith-Stevenson Estate
Architect unknown
Carroll and Bateman Avenues
Demolished

A large Gothic Revival fieldstone cottage, originally known as *Hawthorne Place*, built possibly by Alexander McGregor for J. B. Smith, sold to Eliza Arnold, and thence occupied by the Stevenson family of Philadelphia, *Hawthorne Villa* was set far back on its lot in an English Romantic–style landscape. Howard Augustin Stevenson (1842–1911) was a wholesale druggist with the firm of Bean & Stevenson who married Rosalie C. Hunter, widow of William Hunter Jr. Stevenson became director of the Drug Exchange of Philadelphia and invested in various Philadelphia streetcar companies. His daughter Augusta Rosalie Stevenson (1870–1956) married Rev. Ezekiel Braddin Hamilton, assistant rector of St.

Bartholomew's church, New York, in 1896. Cornelius Vanderbilt II considered Hamilton one of the brightest clergymen in New York and at his request had him preach a famous sermon on divorce at Newport in 1898, which caused a sensation. This property served as the demarcation line between the urban residential fifth ward and the estate district and was thus an inviting target for development. The villa was demolished in 1967 for a naval housing complex, later rental apartments known as Newport Manor, which was subsequently privatized as the Newport Green condominiums.

The Reefs, street facade, ca. 1857

HOUSE N⁰· 38

THE REEFS—WHITNEY COTTAGE *(1853)*
Wolfe-Phinney-Knower-Whitney Estate
Joseph Wells, architect; alterations by Ogden Codman
Bellevue Avenue at Bancroft Avenue
Demolished

Built for Christopher Wolfe (1791–1857) of New York by English-born New York architect Joseph Collins Wells (1814–60), this fine Italianate villa on the cliffs was one of the pre–Civil War showplaces of Newport. Wells had completed the Joseph M. Hart house, *Bienvenu*, on Narragansett Avenue the same year and would go on to build the brownstone Lombard Romanesque Newport Congregational church in 1857. Wolfe and his brother John David Wolfe (1792–1872) were wholesale hardware merchants and real estate developers. The family firm of Wolfe, Dash & Fisher traded mainly with the South, and with the interruption of the Civil War the business was liquidated in 1864. Christopher's niece, John's daughter, was Catherine Lorillard Wolfe, future builder of *Vinland*. The timber-framed summer cottage was of classic Italianate form with projecting central tower entrance, asymmetrical flanking wings adorned with bay windows, bracketed eaves, and wraparound veranda. The new villa was sold in 1858, after Wolfe's death, to Theodore William Phinney (1828–1912) and his wife, Rose Dimond Phinney. Phinney's father, Theodore Phinney (1776–1852), owned three sugar and coffee planta-

Top: *The Reefs (Whitney Cottage), entrance facade, ca. 1930*
Bottom: *garden facade, ca. 1935*

tions in Cuba and brought his family north for the children's education, settling in the old Jaheel Brenton house on Thames Street in 1832. With a growing family of his own, T. W. Phinney engaged Richard Morris Hunt to build a large rough-hewn stone manor house called *Hilltop*, at Carroll and Ruggles Avenues, to which they moved, on its completion, in 1872.

The estate was subsequently purchased by John Knower (1809–92), New York wool merchant, who named it *Sea-Cliffe*. He had developed the habit of summering in Newport with his cousin Abel French (1814–88). Abel's widow, Sarah French, sold the estate in 1896 to newlyweds Harry Payne Whitney (1872–1930) and Gertrude Vanderbilt Whitney (1875–1942). Gertrude, who had grown up at her father's *The Breakers,* took an active interest in the redesign of her new home; *The Reefs* was encased in stucco and renovated with a new ballroom wing by the architect Ogden Codman as *Whitney Cottage*. Soon embarked on a productive career as a sculptor and art patron, Gertrude Vanderbilt Whitney added a Shingle Style sculpture studio on the cliffs, where she studied under the tutelage of Hendrik Christian Andersen. This studio was swept away in the great hurricane that devastated the southern New England coast on September 21, 1938. It was replaced with a yellow brick Moderne style studio by Auguste Noel (1884–1964) of Noel and Miller, architects of the original Whitney Museum, in 1939. On December 20, 1942, while occupied by the family of Mrs. Whitney's sister Gladys, Countess Laszlo Széchényi (1886–1965), the villa caught fire and was severely damaged. The main structure was demolished in 1945; the surviving gatehouse was sold and moved to nearby Ruggles Avenue and the site acquired by Mr. S. Griswold Flagg (Dorothy King) of Radnor, Pennsylvania. The Flagg family in turn sold the estate, with Gertrude Whitney's surviving studio, to New York stockbroker Reginald Bulkeley Rives (1890–1957) and his wife, Gabrielle Warren Rives (1895–1971), daughter of Whitney Warren. In 1953, the Rives had a Georgian-style red brick house built on the lower slope of the lot by architect Frederick Rhinelander King and resurrected the name of *Sea-Cliffe* for the estate.

The Reefs, street or entrance facade, ca. 1875

The Reefs (Whitney Cottage), dining room, ca. 1898

Reef Point, entrance facade, ca. 1890

HOUSE N⁰· 39

REEF POINT *(1860)*
Yznaga-Ingersoll-Carson Estate
George C. Mason (?)
Yznaga Avenue and the Cliffs
Demolished

This ambitious Italianate timber-framed oceanfront villa was built for Cuban American planter and trader Antonio Yznaga del Valle (1823–92) of New York; Cuba; and Ravenswood Plantation, Louisiana, in whose honor the small private street off the east side of Bellevue Avenue was named. Yznaga came from a landowning family of Basque origins established in Trinidad in southern Cuba; his wife was American, the former Ellen Maria Clement of Ravenswood, Louisiana. The Yznagas' daughter Consuelo (1858–1909) was a childhood friend of Alva Erskine Smith, subsequently Mrs. William K. Vanderbilt, who spent much time in this cottage as a girl. Her attachment to the site led to Alva's returning with Mr. Vanderbilt and buying the former Stout cottage two doors north on Bellevue, on which she built her *Marble House*. Alva Vanderbilt's sister, Mary Virginia Smith (1843–1926) married Consuelo's brother Fernando (1853–1901) in turn, and Alva's daughter Consuelo Vanderbilt was named in her honor following Consuelo Yznaga's 1876 aristocratic marriage to Viscount Mandeville, later Duke of Manchester.

The estate passed in 1868 to Harry Ingersoll (1809–86) and his wife, Sarah Emlen Ingersoll (1810–92) of *Medary*, an estate in greater Philadelphia. The Ingersolls were art collectors and literary, having befriended Charles Dickens and James Fenimore Cooper. Following Mrs. Ingersoll's death, the property was acquired by Robert Niedermark Carson (1844–1907), a retired Philadelphia banker and streetcar developer. The 1904 construction of the Edward C. Knight Jr. estate, *Clarendon Court*, on the Bellevue Avenue frontage of Yznaga Avenue created a large Beaux-Arts house with little land and no ocean view. *Reef Point* was purchased from Carson's heirs by Mr. Knight in February of 1910 to extend the grounds of his estate to the cliffs. The house was pulled down to extend the vista and its site landscaped into the *Clarendon Court* property.

Gull Rock, ca. 1890

HOUSE N⁰· 40

GULL ROCK *(1872)*
McKim-Hunnewell-Shaw-Merriman Estate
Richard Morris Hunt, architect;
George Russell Shaw, Dudley Newton (renovations)
Bellevue and Yznaga Avenues
Demolished

Built by Richard Morris Hunt at the end of Yznaga Avenue in 1872 as the summer residence of New Yorker Robert Vanderburgh McKim (1841–1915), a retired Union army surgeon, and his wife, Mary S. Albert McKim, *Gull Rock* was originally a rambling Stick Style cottage perched on the edge of the cliffs. It was sold in 1876 to Hollis Horatio Hunnewell (1836–84) of Boston, son of the railroad financier and horticulturist Horatio Hollis Hunnewell (1810–1902) and Isabella Pratt Welles Hunnewell, who popularized rhododendrons in the United States and created extraordinary botanical gardens at his estate *Wellesley* outside Boston, after which the city of Wellesley, Massachusetts, was named. Hollis Hunnewell undertook major alterations with his architect, George Russell Shaw, of Shaw & Hunnewell, in 1883, then bequeathed the estate to his daughter, Charlotte Bronson Hunnewell (1872–1961), later Mrs. Victor Sorchan and Mrs. Walton Martin. The estate was subsequently owned by Robert Gould Shaw II (1872–1930) of Boston, son of Quincy Adams Shaw and Pauline Agassiz Shaw. Shaw was first married to Nancy W. Langhorne (1879–1964) then to Mary Hannington (1874–1937). His family had maintained a summer cottage next to the Agassiz estate at Castle Hill in Newport and he had numerous Parkman and Agassiz cousins in the community. Following Shaw's death, *Gull Rock* was acquired by New York attorney Augustine Leftwich Humes (1875–1952), a director of International Business Machines Corporation, and his wife, Elsa Portner Humes. They sold the property to the family of Edward Bruce Merriman (1872–1936) of Providence, investor and founder of Merriman Solidified Oil, and his wife, Helen Abbe Pearce. Acquired in November 1972 by Mr. and Mrs. Claus von Bulow, *Gull Rock* was demolished and its site incorporated into the grounds of adjacent *Clarendon Court*. Following the 1988 sale of the von Bulow estate, the *Gull Rock* site was separated and sold as the setting for a contemporary home.

Gull Rock, aerial view, ca. 1955

Seaverge, salon, ca. 1955

HOUSE N⁰· 41

SEAVERGE (CA. 1850)
Paine-Cook-Gerry-Hartford-Tinney Estate
Original architect unknown; alterations by Peabody & Stearns
Bellevue Avenue at curve
Demolished

A large midnineteenth-century timber-framed cottage built for John
Paine (1793–1852) of the Bank of Troy, New York, *Seaverge* was much
altered and embellished by Henry H. Cook (1821–1905) in 1883 us-
ing the Boston architectural firm of Peabody & Stearns. Cook, a New
York financier and railroad and real estate investor had built an imposing
granite mansion the same year with architect W. Wheeler Smith at the
corner of Seventy-eighth Street and Fifth Avenue, torn down in 1909
for the James B. Duke mansion, followed by a smaller McKim, Mead
& White Renaissance townhouse at 973 Fifth, which he did not live
to see completed. On Cook's death, the Newport estate became the

Top: *Seaverge, (right) aerial, and Rockhurst (left), ca. 1930*
Middle: *Seaverge, garden facade, ca. 1955*
Bottom: *Seaverge, entrance facade, ca. 1955*

summer home of lawyer and social reformer Elbridge Thomas Gerry (1837–1927), commodore of the New York Yacht Club, and his wife, Louisa Matilda Livingston Gerry (1836–1920). The Gerrys had completed a Richard Morris Hunt brick Renaissance château in 1894 at the corner of Fifth Avenue and Sixty-first Street. Daughters Angelica and Mabel (later Mrs. Francis S. E. Drury of *Drury Lodge*) lived with their parents; sons Robert Livingston Gerry, with wife Cornelia Averell Harriman, and Peter Goelet Gerry, U. S. representative and later senator from Rhode Island, with first wife Mathilde Townsend and second wife Edith Stuyvesant Dresser Vanderbilt, lived nearby independently.

On Elbridge T. Gerry's death, the property was sold to Mrs. Edward Vassalio Hartford, the former Henrietta Guerard Pallitzer (1881–1948). Edward V. Hartford (1870–1922) was the son of A&P food-store founder George Huntington Hartford and himself founded the Hartford Suspension Co., which perfected the shock absorber. A widow with two children, Josephine Hartford (1902–92)—later O'Donnell, later Bryce—and Huntington Hartford (1911–2008), Mrs. Hartford married in 1937 Prince Guido Pignatelli (1900–67). In 1948 *Seaverge* was sold to Mrs. Peyton Jaudon van Rensselaer (1871-1956) formerly of *Knight Cottage* on Bellevue Avenue. In 1955, the estate was acquired by Mr. Harold B. Tinney (1900–89), who lived there with his wife, the former Ruth Betzer, and son Donald, until their purchase in 1956 for $25,000 of nearby *Belcourt*. *Seaverge* was sold and in 1957 demolished for subdivision. The Tinney family salvaged significant interior architectural elements for their collection, together with a seahorse weathervane which now tops the stable block at *Belcourt*.

Rockhurst, garden façade, ca. 1923

Rockhurst, gate lodge, ca. 1898

HOUSE N⁰· 42

ROCKHURST *(1891)*
H. Mortimer Brooks–Aspegren-James Estate
Peabody & Stearns, architects
Bellevue Avenue and Ledge Road
Demolished

This local Rocky Farm stone-and-shingle summer residence, built on the site of Mrs. Gardner Brewer's cottage *Finisterre*, for Mrs. Henry Mortimer Brooks of New York and Aiken, South Carolina, was amongst the most château-esque of Peabody & Stearns' Newport cottages. The street facade featured rounded towers with candlesnuffer roofs flanking a central block, with an open arcaded gallery along the second story. The Norman half-timbered garden elevation faced the sea with a broad central veranda. As the Brookses became a social success, a white and gold Louis XV–style ballroom was added off the east side conservatory in the spring of 1896 by Peabody & Stearns with decorator Allard & Sons. Mrs. Brooks (1850–1920) was the former Josephine F. Higgins, daughter of Elias S. Higgins of E. S. Higgins & Co. carpet manufacturers and a director of the C&O Railroad. She married Henry Mortimer Brooks (1847–1937) in 1868 and had three children, a son Reginald (1873–1957), who in 1901 married Phyllis Langhorne, sister of Nancy Langhorne Shaw; and two daughters who both married the sons of neighboring Bellevue Avenue estates: Josephine, Mrs. John Riley Livermore of *Inchiquin,* and Gladys, Mrs. Eugene Van Rensselaer Thayer of *Thayer Cottage.* Following Mrs. Brooks' death in 1920, the 12½-acre estate at the eastern tip of Aquidneck Island was sold to John Aspegren (1876–1924), a Swedish immigrant who on arriving in the United States in 1899, with his brother Adolf, founded Aspegren & Co., a leader in the vegetable oil industry. With his wife, the former Lucille Valentine Bacon, the couple entertained generously and renamed the property *Aspen Hall* during the family's 1922–29 occupancy. In 1930, the property was purchased by Mrs. Walter B. James (née Helen Goodsell Jennings, 1860–1946) of New York, widow of Dr. Walter Belknap James (1858–1927), president of the Jekyll Island Club 1919–27, and daughter of Oliver Burr Jennings (1825–93), Standard Oil investor and brother-in-law of William Rockefeller Jr. Mrs. James' sister, Mrs. Hugh D. Auchincloss (née Emma Brewster Jennings, 1861–1942) lived nearby at *Hammersmith Farm,* and her brother, Oliver Gould Jennings (1865–1936) next door on Bellevue Avenue at *Bellacre* or *Mailands.* In 1944, Mrs. James retired to Southampton, New York, and sold the estate to Frederick H. Prince Jr. (1885–1962), whose father had purchased the nearby *Marble House* in 1932

Rockhurst, entrance facade, ca. 1895

for $100,000. Mr. Prince, a partner with Charles G. West (1890–1962) in a local real estate syndicate, sold *Rockhurst*, then called *Lowlands*, as a development site, choosing to demolish the long-empty main house in September of 1955 for residential subdivision. The gatehouse and gardener's cottage survive and, recently restored by Mr. West's daughter, give an excellent idea of the original scale of the Brooks villa.

Top: *Rockhurst, ca. 1950*
Bottom: *Rockhurst, entrance facade, ca. 1923*

Top: *Mrs. Walter B. James, ca. 1940*

Middle: *Rockhurst, Allard & Sons French ballroom, 1896*

Bottom: *Rockhurst, Aspegren Ball, 1923*

Train Villa (Beachholm), ca. 1890

HOUSE N°· 43

BEACHHOLM *(1869)*
Train-Blair Estate
Cyrus Peckham, builder
Bellevue Avenue at Bailey's Beach
Demolished

Formerly known as the *Train Villa* or *Showandsee*, this was considered the last large mansard-roofed Italianate cottage erected in Newport. Built for Newport real estate promoter Alfred Smith (1809–86), the villa was sold to the once legendary George F. Train (1829–1904) of Boston and was occupied by Train's family while he embarked on numerous adventurous enterprises. Train built the first tramway line in England; organized the clipper ship line that sailed around Cape Horn to San Francisco; set up the Crédit Mobilier bank in America to fund the Union Pacific Railroad, which he had also helped to organize; traveled around the world in eighty days in 1870, possibly inspiring Jules Verne's novel, and repeated the record-breaking voyage twice more at seventy-two and sixty days; ran as an independent for president of the United States in 1872; and was an early funder and supporter of women's rights causes. The estate was subsequently acquired by prominent attorney Woodbury Blair (1853–1932) of New York, son of Abraham Lincoln's postmaster general, Montgomery Blair (1813–83). Badly damaged by fire in the early 1970s, the *Train Villa* was replaced with a smaller contemporary home on the site.

Train Villa (Beachholm), ca. 1947

Train Villa (Beachholm), ca. 1890

Train Villa (Beachholm), ca. 1955

Richard Baker House, aerial view, ca. 1925

Baker Cottage, seen from Bailey's Beach, 1919

Baker Cottage–Westcliff, ca. 1890

RICHARD BAKER JR. HOUSE–WESTCLIFF *(1870)*

Mixter-Baker-Saunders Estate
Richard Morris Hunt, architect
Ledge Road
Demolished

Characteristic of Hunt's early Newport cottages, the *Baker House*, also known as *Westcliff*, was a large asymmetrically planned Stick Style cottage with picturesque verandas and balconies reminiscent of his 1863 Griswold House in Newport. Here, however, Hunt renovated an existing 1854 cottage at the end of the Cliff Walk facing west toward Bailey's Beach that had been built for Boston banker and merchant Charles Mixter (1811–73) and added on contrasting rooflines. These consisted of hipped and gambrel roofs giving way to high-pitched mansard towers, which, while remaining timber-framed, were to be a signal of the architect's evolution toward the château-esque. Occupied by Boston merchant Richard Baker Jr. (1819–75) of 152 Commonwealth Avenue, a partner in the shipping firm of William F. Weld &

Co., his wife Ellen M. Whittemore Baker (1827–96) and their four children, the Baker heirs sold their interest in 1923 to Dr. Truman L. Saunders (1878–1965) and his wife, Elizabeth G. Bacon Saunders (1891–1949), of New York. The house was pulled down and replaced with a "Normandy manor"–style residence in 1929.

Cadwalader Cottage, ca. 1925

HOUSE Nº· 45

CADWALADER COTTAGE *(1853)*
Cadwalader-Magnin Estate
T. D. Spooner, builder
Bellevue Avenue at Ledge Road
Demolished

On land acquired in 1852 from Newport real estate speculator Joseph I. Bailey, General George Cadwalader (1806–79) of Philadelphia, veteran of the Mexican-American War and the Civil War, had Newport builder Thomas D. Spooner erect in 1853 a large, square, timber-framed Victorian cottage. Set in a park-like setting designed by Newport landscape architect Thomas Galvin, the villa remained in the Cadwalader family, passing to the general's nephew John Cadwalader Jr. (1843–1925), who undertook major renovations in 1889 under the direction of Newport architect J. D. Johnston, then to his son John Cadwalader III (1874–1934) through the midtwentieth century. Sold on September 5, 1942, to recent widow Mrs. Felix Marie Joseph Magnin (née Fannie Robb Carvin (1903–81). In 1961, Mrs. Magnin married Chauncey Beasley (1899–1996), the former headmaster of St. Michael's School in Newport from 1939 to 1947 and subsequently at St. George's School in Middletown. The house was demolished following a fire in the following decade. The site was sold in September 1961 to Martha Wadsworth and is now occupied by a contemporary villa known as *Tree Haven* by architect George Henry Warren and a postmodern Gothic-style cottage.

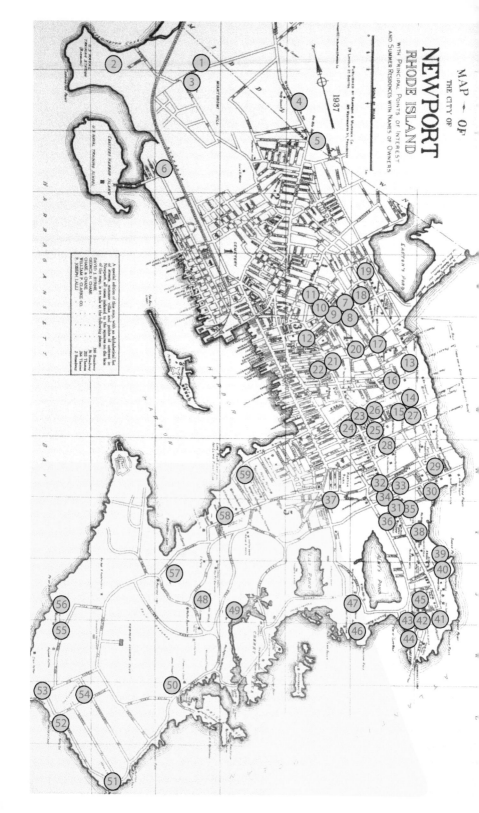

COTTAGES OF OCEAN AVENUE

The Rocks, seaside facade, ca. 1890

The Rocks, entrance facade, ca. 1930

The Rocks, entrance facade, ca. 1920

The Rocks, seen from Bailey's Beach, 1938

HOUSE N^{O.} 46

THE ROCKS *(1868)*
Boit-Clews Estate
John Hubbard Sturgis, architect
Ocean Avenue (west of Bailey's Beach)
Demolished

Built by Boston architect John H. Sturgis of Sturgis & Brigham, architects, for the artist Edward Darley Boit (1842–1915) and his Boston wife, Mary Louisa Cushing Boit (1846–98), *The Rocks* was a rambling timber and granite Queen Anne villa sited on land belonging to Mrs. Boit and her brother Robert Maynard Cushing (1836–1907), children of successful China trader John Perkins Cushing (1787–1862) and his wife, Mary Louisa Gardiner Cushing (1799–1862). Raised on Summer Street in Boston and at *Bellmont*, the vast family country retreat in a part of Watertown, Massachusetts, that subsequently split off and took the township name of Belmont from the estate, the siblings chose to build next to each other on a promontory past Bailey's Beach after the death of their father. The Boits summered here from 1864 to 1871, at which point E. D. Boit, a graduate of Harvard Law School, decided to pursue his artistic training in Italy and Paris. Settling in an apartment at 32, avenue de Friedland, Boit studied with Thomas Couture, became a minor Impressionist, and befriended John Singer Sargent, who in 1882 immortalized the Boit children with his masterpiece *The Daughters of Edward Darley Boit*, now in the Museum of Fine Arts, Boston. While he was living abroad, *The Rocks* was acquired first by retired General Robert Brown Potter (1829–87), son of New York's Bishop Alonzo Potter, and on his death by Boston inventor Thomas J. Montgomery (1849–91). In 1891, *The Rocks* became the summer estate of New York banker and author Henry Clews (1834–1923). The dramatic setting of the house, melting into a boulder-strewn field overlooking the famed Spouting Rock, inspired the artistic aspirations of Henry Clews Jr. (1876–1937), who became a noted sculptor. The house, encased in stucco and much added on to by the Clews family, was demolished in 1948 following the May 1945 sale of the property by Mr. Clews' estate and its grounds incorporated back into the adjoining Robert M. Cushing property, which had remained in the family.

The Rocks, ca. 1895

Harper Cottage ca. 1860

HOUSE NO. 47

SEAFIELD (CA. 1853)
Harper-Field-Warren Estate
Thomas Alexander Tefft, architect
Ocean Avenue at Jeffrey Road
Demolished

Mrs. Catharine "Kitty" Carroll Harper (1778–1861) of Baltimore, daughter of Charles Carroll of Carrollton, signer of the Declaration of Independence, commissioned a timber-framed mansard-roof cottage with continuously shingled walls and roof by then popular Providence architect Thomas Tefft (1826–59). The house occupied an oceanfront parcel of a larger, then isolated, tract of land she had purchased in 1839, through which an access road, now Carroll Avenue, was laid out. Widow of Robert Goodlue Harper (1765–1826), a prominent Maryland lawyer and senator, she had been a friend of the Middleton family since before 1820, and it was possibly their suggestion that brought the Carrolls here. Mrs. Harper shared the cottage with her unmarried daughter, Miss Emily Harper (1812–92), Baltimore's then reigning lady of fashion; together

Seafield, ca. 1950

they contributed significantly to cultural causes in Newport and donated most of the money to erect St. Mary's Church in Newport by the architect Patrick C. Keely (1816–96). Kitty Harper's family circle also included her son Charles' daughter Emily, brought to Newport after the 1837 death of her father. The house was sold by Miss Harper, following her mother's death, to John M. and Elizabeth W.P. Field of Philadelphia who moved the modest Harper house back from the sea and greatly enlarged it with an expansive, gabled, dormered and towered-wing attached to the original cottage. Re-baptized *Seafield*, the estate was sold after 1880 to Newport real estate investor and retired China Trader John N.A. Griswold (1822–1909) and used as a rental property. In 1890, George H. Warren, II (1855–1943), New York stockbroker, whose father occupied the Ray-Warren Cottage on Narragansett Avenue, acquired the property and resided there in season until his death. Following World War II, the house was purchased by a Newport hotelier real estate syndicate and leased seasonally; its last occupants were the owners, crew, families and staff of the British challenging yacht *Sovereign* vying for the 1964 America's Cup. Known jocularly by these tenants as *Mildew Manor*, *Seafield* was sold in 1965 to Howard G. Cushing (1906–79), owner of the adjacent estate, and demolished in 1966. The land has since been split off from the Cushing estate and a new house was built on the site in 2000.

Top: *Beacon Hill House, entrance facade, ca. 1937*
Middle: *Beacon Hill House, aerial view, ca. 1947*
Bottom: *Beacon Hill House, overlooking south lawn, 1957*

Beacon Hill House, ca. 1912

HOUSE N°· 48

BEACON HILL HOUSE *(1910)*
Glover-Addicks-James Estate
Howells & Stokes, architects
Beacon Hill Road
Demolished

Occupying the highest, rockiest hill of Newport, where the marine artist
William Trost Richards frequently painted seascapes, the estate at Beacon Hill, so named for the beacons that were once lit near its crest,
was designed to blend into its natural environment. This naturalistic
concern was in keeping with the recommendations of Frederick Law
Olmsted, H. H. Richardson, and Richard Morris Hunt for the development of this sector of Newport. Their client was John Henry Glover
(1827–1902), New York and Newport real estate developer, and his wife,
Helen LeRoy Glover (1828–1916). With his wife's King family relatives
as partners in the scenic development of this, the King-Glover-Bradley
plat, Glover's sensibilities called for villas built of materials that would
complement the rocky site; plans were accordingly commissioned for

several model houses in 1885 from architects McKim, Mead & White and scenic roads laid out. *Belvoir*, Glover's residence, was erected as a fieldstone house from rocks quarried a few yards away on Hammersmith Road, and nestled amidst boulders with a dramatic vista to the sea. The cottage was sold in 1900 to Delaware gasworks entrepreneur J. Edwards Addicks (1841–1919), a four-time unsuccessful candidate for senator from the state; he placed the property, then known as *Telegraph Hill* for the telegraph operators stationed there to watch and wire results of the offshore New York Yacht Club races, on the market in January 1907. In 1909, the estate was acquired by speculator in copper mines and railroads Arthur Curtiss James (1867–1941) of New York and his wife, Harriet Eddy Parsons James (1868–1941). James had just inherited the lion's share of his father, Daniel Willis James' (1832–1907) $26 million estate and decided to tear the original, narrower house down and build a larger version of gray pudding stone, from the site, with limestone trim, reminiscent of *Belvoir*. The exterior of the resultant *Beacon Hill House*, as designed by Isaac Newton Phelps Stokes, son of Mr. James' cousin Anson Phelps Stokes and partner with John Mead Howells in the architectural firm of Howells & Stokes, was relatively austere; two semicircular

Beacon Hill House, seen from the Blue Garden, ca. 1920

Top:
*Beacon Hill House,
living room,
ca. 1912*

Middle:
*Beacon Hill House,
"della Robbia" room,
ca. 1912;
Beacon Hill House,
drawing room,
ca. 1912*

Bottom: *Beacon Hill
House, hall, ca. 1912*

projections adorned the house on either end, twin Renaissance gabled slightly projecting elevations flanked the central round arch-windowed and wrought-iron porte cochère–adorned central mass. The builder was the Whitney Co. of New York. The interiors, however, organized around a two-story center hall, included fully paneled walnut reception rooms in Louis XVI and Jacobean taste and the "della Robbia" room, with a fountain and vaulted ceiling of Guastavino tiles. Mr. James was commodore of the New York Yacht Club, heir to the Phelps Dodge copper mining interests, and a major western railroad investor; his 218' sail and steam yacht *Aloha* was anchored nearby in Newport harbor and accessed via launch from *Aloha Landing*, a Shingle Style boathouse nestled amidst preexisting estates.

Arthur Curtiss James purchased neighboring *Edgehill*, the former George Gordon King Shingle Style estate (1889) by McKim, Mead & White, in 1911 from Mrs. Herman E. Duryea for the use of his sister-in-law Amelia Parsons Ferry. With this addition, James' property grew to become the largest in Newport at 125 acres, with three villas; a "Swiss Village" model farm by architect Grosvenor Atterbury, known as *Surprise Valley Farm* (1914); elaborate formal gardens used for Mrs. James' musicales, including Frederick Law Olmsted Jr.'s 1913 Blue Garden; and the boathouse. In 1914 Mr. and Mrs. James engaged Allen & Coffens, architects of Boston, to build their new city residence at 39 East Sixty-ninth Street at Park Avenue; a set-back Tennessee marble–clad English neoclassical block, the mansion's interiors were an academic study in the English Renaissance style. With the deaths of Mr. and Mrs. James within three weeks of each other in 1941, the Newport estate was willed to the James Foundation of New York, which in 1951 gifted the houses and real estate to the Roman Catholic diocese of Providence. One of the villas, *Zeerust*, was converted to a convent and novitiate, and a service building was made into an elementary school. The main house was seldom utilized, and in May of 1967, vandals started a fire in *Beacon Hill House*. Gutted, the estate was demolished in August of 1967, and 70 acres were sold for residential development. A fieldstone gatehouse, the carriage house–garage, and boathouse survive as private residences, and the Swiss Village is restored and repurposed as a farm for the conservation of heritage breeds.

Zeerust, garden facade, 1926

HOUSE N⁰. 49

ZEERUST *(1919)*
James-Vos Estate
Grosvenor Atterbury, architect
Brenton Road
Demolished

Built as a guest villa on the old King-Glover parcel for the Arthur Curtiss James estate by family architects Atterbury & Phelps, *Zeerust* was a stuccoed, multigabled English-style country house with artist's studio overlooking Cherry Neck Cove. The summer house was designed and built between 1915 and 1919 explicitly with an artist in mind; James family protégé and portraitist Hubert Vos (1855–1935), who had executed portraits of Mr. James' father, D. Willis James (1909), and of A. C. James himself in 1917. The Dutch-born Vos had garnered fame when he and his Hawaiian-Chinese-American wife, Eleanor Kaikilani Coney Graham (1867–1943, married in 1895), visited China in 1905 to paint the portrait of the Dowager Empress Cixi. From his New York studio at West Sixty-seventh Street, Vos drew the attention of the financial elite of New York and the friendship of Mr. and Mrs. James. Vos paid particular attention to the landscape plans of *Zeerust* drawn up by the Olmsted Brothers, with emphasis on preserving the natural topography and introducing exotic flora encountered from his travels in the Orient.

Following Mr. James' 1941 death, the 13½ acre estate passed to the James Foundation of New York, with provisions made for Mrs. Vos as a beneficiary. With the 1951 gift of the real estate to the Catholic diocese, *Zeerust* was offered by the Diocese of Providence to the Sisters of St. Joseph of Cluny for their use as a novitiate. The sisters founded an elementary school in the fieldstone service buildings of the adjacent James rose garden in 1957. The main house suffered from institutional use with the south wing being truncated for a yellow brick residential block; the south wing comprising entrance facade gable, tower, and studio survived but was demolished three years after sale on the private market by the Sisters of St. Joseph in 2007.

Zeerust, entrance facade, 1926

Avalon, ca. 1910

HOUSE N⁰· 50

AVALON *(1906)*
Rawson-Cushman-Van Alen Estate
Grosvenor Atterbury, architect
Ocean Avenue
Demolished

One of a handful of early-twentieth-century Mediterranean Revival houses in Newport, *Avalon* was built as the summer residence of New York attorney Edward Stephen Rawson (1868–1935) and his wife Elizabeth Pendleton Rogers Rawson (1868–1953), granddaughter of Archibald Rogers of Hyde Park, New York. Architect Grosvenor Atterbury (1869–1956), in his first major Newport commission, to which he would return for an expansion in 1917, indulged in a Spanish Colonial vocabulary of Mission-style pediment, stuccoed walls, red-tiled roof, wrought iron balcony, and arched windows for this rambling one- and two-story L-shaped villa with tower pavilion.

Avalon was sold in 1916 to Vera Charlotte Scott Cushman (1876–1946) of New York, heir to Chicago's Carson, Pirie, Scott department store and wife of New York businessman James Stewart Cushman (1871–1952). A socially prominent woman in Newport and New York, Vera Scott

Cushman also dedicated her life to social service as a promoter of the YWCA. At *Avalon*, she brought Atterbury back for additions and at the same time built a similar Spanish Colonial–themed stucco guesthouse on Hammersmith Road known as *Moorland Lodge* (1916–18), in which Atterbury combined architectural elements used at *Avalon*, such as the picturesquely disposed tower, and elements he would soon use nearby at the Swiss Village, such as a wide arched bridge over the entrance drive.

Following Mr. Cushman's death, *Avalon* was sold in 1952 to James "Jimmy" H. Van Alen (1902–91), founder of the International Tennis Hall of Fame at the Newport Casino and inventor of the tennis tiebreaker scoring system, and his wife, Candace Alig Van Alen (1912–2002). The house was devastated by fire in 1976 and the Van Alens rebuilt by truncating the burnt-out upper stories of the central corps of the house and converting it to a primarily single-story structure. The estate was sold in 2006 following Mrs. Van Alen's death, and given the alterations to the historic architectural fiber of *Avalon*, it was demolished for a new residence and guesthouse in 2009.

Top: *Avalon, ca. 1915*

Bottom: *Avalon, from garden, gouache by Mstislav Dobujinsky, ca. 1920*

The Reef, ca. 1920

THE REEF *(1883)*
Davis-Budlong Estate
John Hubbard Sturgis, architect
Ocean Avenue at Brenton Point
Demolished

The Reef was built at windswept Brenton Point, the southwestern-most tip of Aquidneck Island, by Theodore M. Davis (1838–1915), lawyer, copper magnate, author, collector, and renowned Egyptologist. The Point was named for colonial governor William Brenton (1600–74) whose farm comprised most of this section of Newport. Between 1882 and 1883, the Boston architectural firm of Sturgis & Brigham created an elegant shingle-and-stone-clad Queen Anne villa near the shoreline that was destined to house Davis' collection of Old Master paintings, largely bought through the art consultant Bernard Berenson and later bequeathed to the Metropolitan Museum of Art in New York. Richly paneled reception rooms in Jacobean taste were hung with the painting

Top: *The Reef, ca. 1890*
Middle: *The Reef, garden, ca. 1914*
Bottom: *The Reef, ca. 1920*

collection, and the walled gardens and greenhouses were renowned. Between 1903 and 1912, T. M. Davis wintered on the Nile and was granted a license to dig from the Egyptian government. He discovered the tombs of Queen Hatshepsut, Tuthmosis IV, Siptah, Horemheb, Yuaa, and Thuiu, whose artifacts are now in the collections of the Cairo Museum. Over the years, significant improvements were made to the Davis summer residence; a nephew, architect Theodore Davis Boal, built a new cement stable-garage with cupola bell tower in 1903, and the old 1883 stable was renovated as bungalow servant quarters.

Top:
*The Reef, hall,
ca. 1920*

Bottom:
*The Reef,
drawing room,
ca. 1920*

Following Mr. Davis' death in 1915 and that of his estranged wife, Annie, the same year, protracted litigation involving Mr. Davis' mistress, Emma Andrews, his late wife's cousin, delayed the sale of the eighteen-acre estate until 1923, when the property was purchased by Milton J. Budlong (1869–1941), a pioneer in auto distribution and sales and former president of Packard Motor Car Co. of New York. Mrs. Budlong, the former Jessie Margaret Wilson, initiated an acrimonious divorce in 1926, settled only in 1928, and the property was placed in contention. Once the divorce was settled, Budlong remarried and returned to the estate until his death in 1941. That same year, *The Reef* was requisitioned by the government for installation of World War II antiaircraft gun emplacements and lodgings for gunnery personnel. The house was returned to the family in 1946, but Budlong's heir, Miss Frances Budlong, chose not to take up residency and the house sat empty and the grounds neglected. Vandalized throughout the 1950s, the crumbling villa became a popular rendezvous spot and was set on fire in 1961. The gutted corner tower and adjoining walls were finally demolished on May 25, 1963. The site was acquired by the State of Rhode Island and became Brenton Point State Park in 1976, with the restored Davis-era servants' bungalow renovated as a visitor center and the now derelict stable-garage, popularly known as *The Bells*, serving as a romantic ruin.

The Reef, ca. 1955

Bleak House, ca. 1897

HOUSE N⁰· 52

BLEAK HOUSE *(1895)*
Winans-Perry Estate
Peabody & Stearns, architects; Stone & Carpenter, renovations
Ocean Avenue at Winans Avenue
Demolished

Ross Revillon Winans of Baltimore (1850–1912), son of St. Petersburg–Moscow, Russia, railroad developer Thomas deKay Winans (1820–78) and grandson of railroad pioneer and builder-inventor of rail locomotives Ross Winans (1796–1877), chose Peabody & Stearns, architects, to erect a low-slung Shingle Style villa on an exposed ledge facing Pirate's Cove. Named after Charles Dickens' 1853 novel to continue the tradition of his literary father's so-named 1873 cottage on the site by Richard Morris Hunt (demolished in 1894), *Bleak House* was built as Ross R. Winans' sister Celeste Marguerite Hutton Winans (1855–1925) was erecting (1894–96) the more baronial *Shamrock Cliff*, with Peabody & Stearns, on the site of R. M. Hunt's Arthur Bronson house (1861), a short distance north. Following Ross R. Winans' death, *Bleak House* was sold to Providence utilities magnate Marsden Jaseal Perry (1850–1935) in 1907. Perry lived in the historic John Brown house (1786) in Providence, which he modernized and renovated; he accordingly used his Providence architects, Stone & Carpenter, to embellish the interiors of the Newport residence. The estate remained in the Perry family until badly damaged by the 1938 hurricane. The house sat on the market and was finally demolished in 1948, with salvaged stonework removed by Trappist monks for use in the construction of a new monastery in Spencer, Massachusetts. In 1949, the oceanfront site and service buildings across Ocean Avenue were sold to Newport developer Louis Chartier (1904–1984) for $90,000, and a residential subdivision was begun facing the house's now open and somewhat eroded site.

Bleak House, gates, ca. 1920

Bleak House, cliff side, ca. 1920

Quincy Adams Shaw House–Castle Hill, from Collins Beach, ca. 1875

HOUSE N⁰· 53

CASTLE HILL *(CA. 1874)*
Quincy Adams Shaw Estate
George Russell Shaw, architect
Ocean Avenue
Demolished

On a rise at Castle Hill overlooking the sandy Collins Beach, Quincy Adams Shaw (1825–1908) of Boston and his wife, Pauline Agassiz Shaw (1841–1917), erected shortly after the death of her father, Swiss American Harvard biologist and geologist Louis Agassiz (1807–73), a tall Italianate summer cottage with panoramic views of the sea and bay. Pauline and her marine biologist and copper mine president brother, Alexander Agassiz (1835–1910), had purchased the thirty-acre peninsula and both built family homes, hers on the southern extremity and his on the northern. The architect for both cottages was Mr. Shaw's cousin George Russell Shaw (1848–1937) of the Boston firm of Shaw & Hunnewell. Quincy Adams Shaw, son of Robert Gould Shaw (1776–1853) and Elizabeth W. Parkman (1785–1853), had instigated copper mining investments vetted by his father-in-law and shared many of the same scientific interests as his brother-in-law, Alexander; it may be, however, that he objected to the 1877 construction of a laboratory on the cliffs at Alexander's home which brought groups of Harvard students to the estate for research. In any case the Shaw cottage was demolished by 1880 and the land surrendered to Alexander Agassiz. Quincy and Pauline Shaw had other cottages, however, at their disposal; his reclusive aunt, Eliza Parkman, whose husband, George Parkman, was brutally murdered in a much publicized 1849 case, maintained a villa on Bellevue Avenue in front of George Bancroft's *Rosecliff*, and the Shaws' son, Robert Gould Shaw II, would later own *Gull Rock* on Yznaga Avenue. The site of the Pauline Agassiz and Quincy Adams Shaw cottage is today an overgrown field.

Bateman's Hotel, veranda, ca. 1930

HOUSE N⁰· 54

BATEMAN'S *(CA. 1755)*
Collins-Bateman-Davis Estate
Architect unknown
Commonwealth Avenue
Demolished

The circa 1786–90 house of Governor John Collins (1717–95) was the
focal point of the Collins country estate and farm known as Brenton
Neck. Bordered by treeless farm and grazing land owned by the Brenton
family, the fields were worked by tenant farmers, including the ambitious Seth Bateman (1802–87). By 1837 Bateman and his wife, the former Elizabeth Peckham, realized that the surrounding scenery might
attract summer visitors and leased the Collins house as a boardinghouse-
hotel. Adding improved amenities and extensive additions to the Collins
house, success followed and Seth Bateman bought the main house and
adjacent fields in 1848 and operated it as *Bateman's Hotel*. By 1860, the

Bateman's Hotel, aerial view, ca. 1930

colonial structure was encased in additions and wings; the old orchard became a grove destined to find favor as an excursion spot for coaching meets, formal picnics, and rustic dances. *Bateman's* became synonymous with the Newport summer colony's lifestyle. Set back from the road, behind ancient drystone walls, the grounds were renowned for their picturesque quality, which included a full-scale 1867 replica, built as a water tower, of the Old Stone Mill in Newport's Touro Park.

Following Seth's death the property was assumed by his younger brother Luther Bateman (1807–91) and then passed to his grand-nephew W. Sidney Bateman (1864–1948) who took over operations of the hotel by 1892 and managed it following purchase in 1893 by sportsman Edmund W. "Ned" Davis (1853–1908), heir to the Perry Davis Pain Killer fortune. Davis was a member of several exclusive Newport area sports-fishing clubs and operated the property along its traditional lines. *Bateman's* was sold by the Davis family only in 1947 to Newport preservationist John Perkins Brown (1905–82). With funding provided by the Misses Edith

(1870–1966) and Maude (1873–1951) Wetmore of *Château-sur-Mer* and others, a restoration was planned to strip the *Bateman's Hotel* complex back to its eighteenth-century core. With the death of Miss Maude Wetmore and the scarcity of funding, J. Perkins Brown sold the property before work was much advanced to local developer Louis Chartier (1904–84) for $13,000 in 1957. *Bateman's Hotel* burned mysteriously on February 24, 1959, and the ruins were cleared for the Chartier Circle subdivision. The historic Governor Collins burial ground survives.

Bateman's Hotel, ca. 1895

Bateman's Hotel, 1957

Top: *Sunset Ridge from Narragansett Bay, ca. 1948*
Bottom: *Sunset Ridge with circular drive, greenhouses, and cutting gardens,
across Ridge Road, aerial view, ca. 1950*

Sunset Ridge, ca. 1888

HOUSE N°· 55

SUNSET RIDGE *(1877)*
Low-Ledyard Estate
George Champlin Mason, architect
Ridge Road
Demolished

Built by the very social Newport cottage architect George Champlin Mason, *Sunset Ridge* was the timber-framed Italianate cottage summer residence of prominent retired China trade merchant Abiel Abbot Low (1811–93), founder of A. A. Low & Bros. of New York. Set at the top of a ridge overlooking the East Passage of Narragansett Bay and the mouth of Newport Harbor, the house's broad west-facing veranda provided romantic sunset views. Low Library (1897) at Columbia University was erected in memory of A. A. Low by his son, Seth. Inherited by Seth Low (1850–1916), educator, diplomat, president of Columbia University, former mayor of Brooklyn, and second mayor of greater New York City (1901–03), the estate remained in the family until its purchase by Lewis Cass Ledyard (1851–1932), prominent attorney, counsel to J. P. Morgan, and president of the New York Bar Association, in 1905. The property was joined by Ledyard with that of *Broadlawns*, built in 1866 for A. A. Low's brother Josiah Orne Low (1821–95), to the south. To reduce tax valuations, *Sunset Ridge* was demolished in 1955.

Armsea Hall, garden facade, ca. 1914

Armsea Hall, aerial view, ca. 1955

Armsea Hall, garden facade, ca. 1940

HOUSE № 56

ARMSEA HALL *(1901)*
Greene-Hoffman-Johnson-Mawer-Douglas Estate
F. L. V. Hoppin, architect
Ridge Road
Demolished

A large porticoed Palladian villa dominating the lower East Passage of
Narragansett Bay, *Armsea Hall* was New York architect Francis Laurens
Vinton Hoppin's (1867–1941) Beaux-Arts Newport masterpiece. Designed for the architect's cousin, General Francis Vinton Greene (1850–
1921), New York police commissioner, Niagara-Ontario utilities president, and a member of the Greene family of Rhode Island, the villa's
neoclassical central core was flanked by two lower projecting wings
with Doric colonnades. The estate, accessed via a tree-lined *allée*, with
a separate service drive terminating in a Palladian stable, was originally
the site of the small cottage and stable of Harriet Newel Phelps Pond
(1815–92), Mrs. Charles F. Pond. Mrs. Pond was the daughter of New
York philanthropist Anson Green Phelps, and Mr. Pond was president

of the New York and New Haven Railroad. As subsequently developed by Hoppin, the estate included notable rose gardens and landscaping by the Olmsted Brothers. Within two years of construction, the property passed to Charles Frederick Hoffman Jr. (1856–1919), son of Rev. Dr. Charles Frederick Hoffman of New York and Zelia Krumbhaar Hoffman (1867–1929), daughter of G. R. Preston, president of the Hibernian National Bank of New Orleans, in exchange for the Hoffmans' property *Edgecliff* on Yznaga Avenue. A founder and president of the Newport Garden Club, Mrs. Hoffman created a series of celebrated rose arbors with views to Narragansett Bay. Subsequently inherited by Mrs. Aymar Johnson, the former Marian K. Hoffman (1901–81), the estate was leased for a number of years, lastly by the Marquis and Marquise de Cuevas, a granddaughter of J. D. Rockefeller. It was sold in 1945 by Mrs. Johnson for $14,000 to Colin Drummond Mawer (1875–1965), a Brooklyn olive oil manufacturer and his wife, the former Gertrude Bell Hummell (1890–1965), a native of Newport. *Armsea Hall* was purchased next in 1952 by Newport sportsman Barclay Kountze Douglas (1909–91). Known as *Annandale Farm*, this palatial estate, abutting the Auchincloss family's *Hammersmith Farm*, childhood summer home of

Armsea Hall, hydrangea walk, 1914

Jacqueline Bouvier Kennedy, was leased as a summer White House in 1963. President Kennedy intended to use the estate for his planned August 1964 summer holiday. His assassination precluded occupancy and Armsea Hall was sold in 1965 for $150,000 for conversion to a resort. In 1967, the property was purchased at a mortgagee sale for $195,000 and in 1968 was sold a final time for $212,000 for potential residential subdivision. The villa was demolished in 1969 and modern homes subsequently built on a portion of the property; the site of the main house remains open space.

Armsea Hall, ca. 1948

Armsea Hall, west facade, 1963

Armsea Hall, sheep grazing on east lawn, 1957

Armsea Hall, view up bay from terrace walk, 1951

Vedimar, ca. 1930

HOUSE N°. 57

VEDIMAR *(1910)*
Frissell-James-Manice Estate
Atterbury & Phelps, architects
Harrison Avenue
Demolished

Set atop a rocky outcropping at the end of a long entrance drive over-looking the open moors, *Vedimar* was a stucco-over-timber-frame, Spanish Mediterranean Revival villa built as a summer residence for Dr. Lewis Fox Frissell (1872–1934), teacher of clinical medicine at Columbia University and medical director of St. Luke's Hospital, New York. L. F. Frissell was the son of Algernon Sydney Frissell, founder and president of the Fifth Avenue Bank of New York and a cousin of Arthur Curtiss James, who owned the land and title to the house. Frissell's second wife, Antoinette Wood Montgomery Frissell (1871–1931), was a popular socialite and their daughter Antoinette "Toni" Frissell (1907–88), later Mrs. Francis Bacon III, became a celebrated photographer. Their architects, Grosvenor Atterbury and Stowe Phelps, were the architects of choice for the Phelps family, to which the Frissells belonged.

Following the deaths of Dr. and Mrs. Frissell, the estate was returned to Arthur Curtiss James to be incorporated into his surrounding landholdings and used as a guest villa. In 1911, James had acquired the nearby George Gordon King estate, *Edgehill*, and presented it to his wife's niece, Amelia Parsons Ferry (1863–1945), as a summer home; she was the wife of Ebenezer Hayward Ferry (1864–1940), an officer in the family's Phelps Dodge Corporation and vice president of Hanover Bank. The Ferrys' daughter Harriet Ferry Manice (1891–1975), Mrs. William DeForest Manice, would inherit *Edgehill* from her parents and in 1945 paid $50,000 to the James Foundation for the Swiss Village and *Vedimar* to unite the properties into an almost-fifty-two-acre parcel. Following Mrs. Manice's death, the entire property was sold in 1975 to a rehabilitation center. Following auction of its contents, *Vedimar* was demolished the same year to facilitate institutional development of the site. That institution was sold and a successor went into receivership; the tract was auctioned in 1998. Fortunately, two private Newport preservationists bought the complex; in 1999, clinic buildings and parking lots were removed and the Swiss Village rehabilitated as a farm for the preservation of heritage breeds, incorporating the site of *Vedimar*.

Vedimar, living room, 1974

Vedimar, dining room, 1974

Pen Craig, entrance facade, ca. 1925

Pen Craig, ca. 1955

PEN CRAIG *(1865)*

Jones-Webster Estate
Architect unknown
Harrison Avenue
Demolished

Pen Craig was built as an informal timber-framed chalet-type summer cottage overlooking Newport Harbor by George Frederic Jones (1810– 1900) and his wife, Lucretia Stevens Rhinelander Jones (1824–1901), parents of the author Edith Newbold Jones Wharton (1862–1937), who spent her formative childhood summers here. After her 1885 marriage, until the 1893 purchase of *Land's End* on Ledge Road, Edith Jones Wharton resided in a dependency across Harrison Avenue known as *Pen Craig Cottage*, later *Auton House*, home and studio of architect F. L. V. Hoppin. On Mrs. Jones' 1901 death, the estate was acquired by New York attorney Hamilton Fish Webster (1861–1939), grandson and namesake of Hamilton Fish (1808–93), New York governor and U.S. secretary of state, and his wife, Lina Post Webster (1866–1951), who "Tudorized" and extended the cottage. Following the death of Mrs. Webster, the house was sold at auction on July 17, 1956, to a group of local real estate investors, and *Pen Craig* was demolished for residential subdivision. A circa 1900 brick and clapboard carriage house survives, as does *Pen Craig Cottage*.

Harbourview, garden facade, ca. 1897

Harbourview, ca. 1910

HOUSE N°· 59

HARBOURVIEW *(1865)*
Merrill-Phoenix-French Estate
George Champlin Mason, architect
Wellington Avenue at Ida Lewis Yacht Club
Demolished

Harbourview was built on a hilltop overlooking the inner harbor for attorney and planter Ayres P. Merrill II (1826–83) and his wife, Jane Sur-
get Merrill (1829–66) of *Elms Court*, Natchez, Mississippi, by the active
Newport architect George Champlin Mason. *Harbourview* was one of
the most ambitious of Mason's Italianate cottages and was renovated by
him for two subsequent owners. The Merrills were leaders of the Natchez set in antebellum Newport, which also included the Duncan and
Mercer families. Following the Civil War, Merrill moved to New York
and was appointed ambassador to Belgium by President U. S. Grant.
In 1876, the house was acquired by the New York collector, genealo-
gist, and traveler Stephen Whitney Phoenix (1839–81), a friend of the
Pumpelly family. Following Mr. Phoenix's death in 1881, the property was sold to New York lawyer and banker Francis Ormond French

(1837–93); his daughter, Ellen "Elsie" Tuck French (1879–1948), married Alfred Gwynne Vanderbilt (1877–1915) in Newport in 1901, and their son, William H. Vanderbilt III (1901–81), later became governor of Rhode Island (1939–41). Following her divorce from A. G. Vanderbilt in 1908, Ellen Tuck French Vanderbilt received title to *Harbourview* from her mother Ellen T. French (1838–1915) in 1911. In 1919 she married Paul Fitzsimmons, continuing to reside at *Harbourview* until her own death there in 1948. Elsie F. Vanderbilt Fitzsimmons' grand-niece and namesake Ellen Tuck French (1915–74) married John J. Astor V of *Chetwode* in 1934. Governor W. H. Vanderbilt inherited the estate in 1948 and sold it in 1951; the house was almost immediately demolished for residential subdivision. An elegant brick and limestone boundary wall, gateposts, and terrace survive.

NOTES

UNPUBLISHED SOURCES:

Archives of The Preservation Society of Newport County,
424 Bellevue Avenue, Newport, R.I. 02840

Land Evidence Records of Newport, R.I., City Hall, Broadway,
Newport, R.I. 02840

New York Times Archives

Newport Daily News Archives, Malbone Road, Newport, R.I.
02840

PUBLISHED SOURCES:

Amory, Cleveland. "The Crucial Battle of Modern Newport," *New
York Times* Magazine, 2 September 1962, pp. 128–30.

Annuaire of the Newport Garden Club, 1914, privately published,
Newport, R.I., 1915.

Architecture, vol. XIV, no. 6, December 1906.

"Country Houses & Gardens," *The Spur*, 15 November 1919.

"Fifty Glimpses of Newport," Rand, McNally & Co., New York,
1897.

James, Henry. *The American Scene*, Harper & Brothers, New York,
1907.

"*Life* Visits a Fading Newport," *Life*, 16 October 1944.

Map of the City of Newport, 1937, Sampson & Murdock Co.,
Providence, R.I., 1937.

Mason, George Champlin Sr. *Newport and Its Cottages*, Rand,
Avery & Co., Boston, 1875.

New York Times, 28 June 1962, p. 33.

Van Rensselaer, Mary King. *Newport Our Social Capital*, J. B.
Lippincott Co., Philadelphia, 1905.

CREDITS

FRONT / BACK COVERS

Front: *Rockhurst, garden facade, T. E. Geisler Photographer; ca. 1923; The Preservation Society of Newport County.* **Back:** *Whiteholme, entrance allée, Alman & Co. Photographers, ca. 1905; The Preservation Society of Newport County.*

FRONTISPIECE

Chetwode garden façade from the fountain basin, ca. 1935; The Preservation Society of Newport County.

INTRODUCTION

Page 8: *Market Square, Newport waterfront, ca. 1890; The Preservation Society of Newport County.*
Page 9: *Ocean House Hotel (burned 1898), Briskham Jackson Photographer, ca. 1890; The Preservation Society of Newport County.* **Page 10:** *Bancroft Cottage, Rosecliff, Clarence Stanhope Photographer, ca. 1890; The Preservation Society of Newport County. Merritt Cottage, The Elms, later E. J. Berwind, Clarence Stanhope Photographer, ca. 1890; The Preservation Society of Newport County. Oakland Farm, entrance facade, Wurts Brothers Photographers, 1906; The Preservation Society of Newport County. Oakland Farm, garden facade, Wurts Brothers Photographers, 1906; The Preservation Society of Newport County.* **Page 11:** *Oakland Farm, riding ring, Wurts Brothers Photographers, 1906; The Preservation Society of Newport County.*

THE COTTAGES

Page 14: *F. W. Andrews House, ca. 1895; courtesy of Shepley, Bulfinch, Richardson and Abbott.*
Page 16: *Castlewood drawing room. Photograph by Floyd E. Baker, 1919; The Preservation Society of Newport County.*
Page 16: *Castlewood, garden facade, Alman & Co. Photographers, 1906; The Preservation Society of Newport County.*
Page 17: *Castlewood, entrance facade, Alman & Co. Photographers, ca. 1920; The Preservation Society of Newport County.*
Page 18: *Castlewood, entrance hall, Alman & Co. Photographers, 1906; The Preservation Society of Newport County.*
Page 18: *Castlewood, dining room, Alman & Co. Photographers, 1906; The Preservation Society of Newport County.*
Page 18: *Castlewood, salon, Alman & Co. Photographers, 1906; The Preservation Society of Newport County.*
Page 19: *Residence of E. S. Philbrick, engraving, James R. Osgood & Co., 1876; The Preservation Society of Newport County.*
Page 20: *John Bannister House, east elevation, 1950, Daniel Jones Photographer; The Preservation Society of Newport County.*
Page 21: *John Bannister House, Meservey Photographer, 1947; The Preservation Society of Newport County.*
Page 22: *Dudley Place, ca. 1920; The Preservation Society of Newport County.*
Page 24: *Dudley Place, ca. 1910, color postcard; The Preservation Society of Newport County.*
Page 25: *Hunter/Dunn-Cloyne House, ca. 1914, color postcard; The Preservation Society of Newport County*

Page 26:   *Hunter-Dunn Estate as St. Michael's School, 1940; The Preservation Society of Newport County.*

Page 30:   *Whitehall, ca. 1900; The Preservation Society of Newport County.*

Page 30:   *Whitehall, ca. 1930; The Preservation Society of Newport County.*

Page 31:   *Whitehall, ca. 1897; Clarence Stanhope Photographer; The Preservation Society of Newport County.*

Page 33:   *The Corners, Ernst Studio Photography, ca. 1935; The Preservation Society of Newport County.*

Page 34:   *T. G. Appleton House, ca. 1875; The Preservation Society of Newport County.*

Page 36:   *Appleton House-Fair Haven, west facade, ca. 1912; The Preservation Society of Newport County.*

Page 36:   *Appleton House-Fair Haven, street facade, ca. 1912; The Preservation Society of Newport County.*

Page 37:   *Richardson Cottage, ca. 1875, Joshua Appleby Williams Photographer; by courtesy of the Robert N. Dennis Collection of Stereoscopic Views, Miriam and Ira D. Wallach Division of Arts, Prints and Photographs, The New York Public Library, Astor, Lenox and Tilden Foundations.*

Page 38:   *Caldwell House, interior, ca. 1890; by courtesy of Historic New England.*

Page 40:   *Hilltop, ca. 1890; by courtesy of The Newport Historical Society, P98*

Page 42:   *Gammell Cottage, ca. 1910; The Preservation Society of Newport County.*

Page 44:   *H. A. C. Taylor Residence, Ticknor & Co., 1887; The Preservation Society of Newport County.*

Page 45:   *H. A. C. Taylor House, ca. 1910; The Preservation Society of Newport County.*

Page 46:   *H. A. C. Taylor House, ca. 1947, Meservey Photographer; The Preservation Society of Newport County.*

Page 46:   *H. A. C. Taylor House, portico, Meservey Photographer, 1947; The Preservation Society of Newport County.*

Page 47:   *Fearing Cottage, ca. 1875; The Preservation Society of Newport County.*

Page 48:   *Fearing Cottage, Croquet Party, ca. 1865; The Preservation Society of Newport County.*

Page 49:   *Sheldon Cottage, ca. 1875; The Preservation Society of Newport County.*

Page 50:   *Beach Cliffe, ca. 1875; The Preservation Society of Newport County.*

Page 53:   *Linden Gate, ca. 1947, Meservey Photographer; The Preservation Society of Newport County*

Page 54:   *Linden Gate, entrance facade, Clarence Stanhope Photographer, ca. 1880; The Preservation Society of Newport County.*

Page 54:   *Linden Gate, garden facade, ca. 1897; The Preservation Society of Newport County.*

Page 55:   *Linden Gate, reception room, ca, 1883; The Preservation Society of Newport County.*

Page 56:   *Linden Gate; stair and entrance hall, 1951; The Preservation Society of Newport County.*

Page 56:   *Linden Gate, east or garden facade with music room, 1969; The Preservation Society of Newport County.*

Page 57:   *Pumpelly Cottage, ca. 1885; The Preservation Society of Newport County.*

Page 58:   *Pumpelly Cottage, ca. 1890, Clarence Stanhope Photographer; by courtesy of The Newport Historical Society, P9664.*

Page 59:   *Ladd Villa, ca. 1897; The Preservation Society of Newport County.*

Page 62:   *Stone Villa, ca. 1957; The Preservation Society of Newport County.*

Page 62:   *Stone Villa, gouache by Mstislav Dobujinsky, 1949; The Preservation Society of Newport County.*

Page 63:   *Stone Villa, ca. 1920; The Preservation Society of Newport County.*

Page 66:   *Stone Villa, gates, ca. 1955; The Preservation Society of Newport County.*

Page 67:   *Paran Stevens Villa, ca. 1890; The Preservation Society of Newport County.*

Page 68:   *Stevens Villa as Buckingham House Hotel, ca. 1912; The Preservation Society of Newport County.*

Page 70:   *Lady Paget as Cleopatra, 1897; The Preservation Society of Newport County.*

Page 71:   *Arleigh, ca. 1910; The Preservation Society of Newport County.*

Page 73:   *Villa Rosa, garden facade, Alman & Co. Photographers, 1904; The Preservation Society of Newport County.*

Page 74:   *Villa Rosa, courtyard and entrance facade, Alman & Co. Photographers, 1904; The Preservation Society of Newport County.*

Page 74:   *Villa Rosa, entrance gate and forecourt, ca. 1930, Ernst Studio Photography; The Preservation Society of Newport County.*

Page 75:   *Villa Rosa, ballroom, Alman & Co. Photographers, 1904; The Preservation Society of Newport County.*

INDEX TO THE COTTAGES

CPSIA information can be obtained
at www.ICGtesting.com
Printed in the USA
BVHW02s0237270618
520105BV00015BA/186/P